THE DNA
OF JESUS CHRIST

GOD'S TRACEABLE IDENTITY

WILLIAM L. "Sonny" PAYNE, JR.

ISBN 978-0-9891562-0-2

Published by Pure Gold Enterprises, P. O. Box 4764, Maryville, TN 37802.

Scripture quotations marked KJ are from the King James Version of the Bible.

Scripture quotations marked NKJ are from the New King James Version of the Bible. Copyright 1979, 1980, 1982. Thomas Nelson Inc., Publishers.

Scripture quotations marked Amplified are from the Amplified Bible. Old Testament copyright 1965, 1987 by the Zondervan Corporation. The Amplified New Testament copyright 1958, 1987 by the Lockman Foundation. Used by permission.

Printed in the United States of America on acid-free paper.

BookLocker.com, Inc.
2013

First Edition

Thanks and Appreciation

First, I want to thank my Heavenly Father, my Savior and Lord, Jesus Christ, and the precious Holy Spirit who guided me through this entire project. You are forever faithful!

To my best friend on earth, my wife, Reva Jo, whose counsel, prayers, patience, love and proofreading have been invaluable for the completion of this project.

To Rebekah Hammond. What a friend you are, and what a journey we have had over the last twenty-four years. Thank you for everything.

To Mike and Maria Dixon. Your love, prayers, support, and belief in Reva and me have been so important. Mike, thank you for insisting that I not delay in getting this book out.

To two amazing prayer warriors: our precious daughter, Ami Elizabeth, and her husband Christopher, and our son Timothy, and his wife Bonnie. To all who have prayed for us, I want to say "Thank you," from the bottom of my heart. Reva and I are so blessed.

Last, but not least, to our seven grandchildren: Elizabeth, Jonathan, Catherine Jo, Isaiah, Laura Beth, Maisie, and Asa. I leave this book as a legacy to you of my love for God and for you and a compass in helping direct your lives. May you forever love and serve Him.

ACKNOWLEDGMENTS

I want to thank my sister, Pamela Archer, and her husband Charles, for all their help, love, prayers, and suggested changes in getting this book completed.

I also want to thank my dear friend and fellow minister Gordon Dunahoe for his critique of the manuscript and suggested changes that were important in clarifying several issues.

Lori Steinbach, thank you for the final edit on my manuscript. You are truly a gift from God and were there at the right time to help bring everything together for publishing.

Lastly, I want to thank all the ministries, authors, and publishers who allowed me to use excerpts from your books, websites, newsletters, and periodicals and helped make this book what it is. I could not have done it without you.

TABLE OF CONTENTS

THANKS AND APPRECIATION III

ACKNOWLEDGMENTS V

TABLE OF CONTENTS VII

PREFACE XIII

CHAPTER 1 - EVIDENCE: THE CASE FOR GOD 1

    NEW AGE THINKING 2

    EVIDENCE OF THE ONE TRUE GOD: THE BIBLE 2

    ETERNAL 3

    CREATOR 4

    THE FOOLISHNESS OF ATHEISM 6

    EVOLUTION VS CREATIONISM 7

    THE MORAL LAW 8

    THE LAWS OF NON-CONTRADICTION AND THE
        EXCLUDED MIDDLE 10

    CREATURE WORSHIP 11

    THE DISCOVERY OF DNA 14

CHAPTER 2 - THE ORIGIN OF SIN AND EVIL 15

    ANGELIC CREATION 15

    A HEAVENLY WAR 17

    HEAVEN'S HALLS STAINED 21

    ANGELS AND DNA 22

    ANGELIC SWORDS 24

    BLOOD: THE FOOD OF DEMONS 27

CHAPTER 3 - A LEVEL PLAYING FIELD................31

SIGNS IN THE HEAVENS 31
SATAN'S DEATH KNELL 33
THE FORBIDDEN FRUIT 33

CHAPTER 4 - THE PROMISED SEED 39

THE ENMITY...41
THREE-FOLD ASPECT OF MESSIAH 43
JEWISH THOUGHT ON GENESIS 3:15 46

CHAPTER 5 - THE BLOOD CRIES OUT 49

BORNEO BLOOD BROTHERHOOD 52
BLOOD COVENANTING..........................53
THE RIGHT OFFERING...........................54
LIVING BLOOD 57
THE RIGHTEOUS VINDICATED................58
JERUSALEM CLEANSED..........................59
ANGOLA PRISON 60
WHAT ABOUT YOUR FUTURE? 63

CHAPTER 6 - SOMEONE IS COMING.................65

THE GODLY SEED.................................66
A FLOOD TO SAVE 68
THE TENTS OF SHEM 72
A KINGLY LINEAGE 75

CHAPTER 7 DNA AND THE VIRGIN BIRTH 80

DNA 83
TYPES OF CONCEPTION........................84
LIFE IN THE WOMB..............................90
A BODY FOR MESSIAH..........................93

PART II: THE VIRGIN BIRTH...**95**

CHAPTER 8 - BORN TO DIE...**101**

THE TEMPTATIONS...106
SIGNS OF THE CROSS 108
    The CRUX *108*
    Laminin...*108*
    Tabernacle *109*
    The tav *111*
    Whirlpool Galaxy...*113*
    Washington D.C....*114*
SACRIFICIAL BLOOD 115

CHAPTER 9 - WAS HE REAL, AND DID HE DIE? **121**

    Jesus Christ, a Real Historical Figure.................................*121*
    Non-Biblical Sources For Jesus' Historicity: Flavius
        Josephus *122*
    Cornelius Tacitus...*123*
    Letter of Mara Bar-Sereapion *123*
    Plinius Secundus,...*123*
    Biblical Sources for Jesus' Historicity: Polycarp *124*
    Origen..*124*
    Irenaeus..*124*
JESUS CHRIST'S CRUCIFIXION AND DEATH..................125
SHROUD OF TURIN..128
TEN PROPHETIC SCRIPTURES FULFILLED
    REGARDING JESUS' DEATH..131

CHAPTER 10 - THE RESURRECTION **133**

JESUS' CLAIMS OF HIS RESURRECTION.........................133
JESUS' RESURRECTION..135

SHROUD OF TURIN AND JESUS' RESURRECTION 138
The first photograph of the Shroud in 1898 139
The blood stains on the Shroud 139
Dr. Accetta's experiment confirms radiation 140
The X-ray appearance of the anatomical hands on the
Shroud 140
Jesus' post-Resurrection appearances 141
TESTIMONIES OF HIGHLY INFLUENTIAL MEN 142

CHAPTER 11 - YOUR ETERNAL DESTINY **145**

IMMORTAL BEINGS 146
A NEW BIRTH 147
TWO RESURRECTIONS 150
Resurrection of the Righteous 151
A Prepared Place 153
Resurrection of the ungodly 155
DISCERNING THE LIGHT 157
How to discern the great light 157

CHAPTER 12 - CHRIST'S SOON RETURN **159**

SIGNS OF CHRIST'S RETURN 159
I. The restoration of Israel as a nation 160
The Balfour Declaration 161
Middle East Conflict 162
Spiritual Conflict 163
II. The coming rebuilt Temple 165
Registering of Levites and Kohanim 166
Sanhedrin 166
The Priesthood DNA 167
The days ahead 169

CONCLUSION **173**

NOTES 175

BIBLIOGRAPHY 181

PREFACE

This book was born out of a simple question that was asked of me one morning at breakfast by a friend of mine. A few of us had gathered in Fredericksburg, VA, for a weekend of prayer, seeking the Lord on some specific directions regarding each of our lives. My friend said, "Sonny, what happened to Adam and Eve when they ate the apple?" My first response was that they disobeyed God's Word. Second, there was something in the forbidden fruit that had a substance of some kind in it that changed their blood chemistry and caused physical death, not an instant death but a death that caused the body to begin to decay and die over time. What substance within the fruit was so powerful that it caused the first two sinless, perfect human beings, created in God's image, to change so dramatically that it altered the history of man forever? To find the answer, I began an in-depth study on the subject.

Years ago, I wrote a book on God's blood covenants with man called *Bought with a Price*, so I was rather familiar with the importance of human blood and its effects on man's eternal destiny. As I delved into these new studies, I began to gain a greater understanding of human blood, its DNA, and the impact it has on the choices we make in life. From my new insights, I wrote an article on Jesus' virgin birth, which I put on my web site www.newgateministries.com. It brought the greatest response of anything I had ever written. It was that article which let me know I had to write this book and show

xiii

the importance of blood and DNA, especially the DNA of Jesus Christ, and the physical and spiritual aspects of the blood.

What causes human beings to excitedly attend sporting events that have a tendency to cause bloodshed (such as boxing, hockey, pro wrestling, dog fights, and other events of like nature), yet run to the aid of someone who has had an accident and is losing blood, to try and stop the bleeding? It is paradoxical. The blood is mysterious yet necessary, not only for physical life but also for spiritual life. In this book I will attempt to unlock the secrets to the mysteries of the blood, give a clear picture of the beauty and majesty of Jesus Christ, show why His DNA was not from human parents, and explain why His blood is the most important element regarding man's eternal destiny. May you find peace, comfort, and assurance reading this book, knowing that if you put your trust in Jesus Christ, your future is secure in Him and He will never leave you or forsake you. He is faithful!

Author: William L. "Sonny" Payne, Jr.

CHAPTER 1
EVIDENCE: THE CASE FOR GOD

"Before the mountains were brought forth, or ever thou hadst formed the earth and the world, even from everlasting to everlasting, thou art God." Psalm 90:2

Virtually every issue facing society today directly affects the human blood system, whether it be sickness, disease, drugs, sex, alcohol, war, worry, fear, hate, jealousy, joy, peace, or love; therefore, we want to begin our journey with the understanding that the blood and DNA of man and of Jesus Christ are the two most important subjects of this book. In our journey, we will discover the great importance of blood covenanting, how God could have a Son without a consort, how God's Son could come to earth as a man, and how the blood and DNA of Jesus Christ was not from an earthly father and mother. This journey will be exciting as we delve into the mysteries of God, His love and compassion for His creation, and His miracle-working power in order to bring about the fullness of His Plan of redemption, to usher in an everlasting peace throughout His universe, and ultimately to dwell in the midst of His highest creation — man.

The two founding principles on which Christianity is based — the Virgin Birth and the Resurrection of Jesus Christ — are either true, or millions of His followers have been greatly deceived. My desire is to put these issues to rest with absolute facts.

NEW AGE THINKING

In an age of postmodernism, the new age movement, paganism, and secular humanism, many people are looking for answers to life, trying to figure out why they exist, what their purpose is for living, and if there really is a God. Three of the latest bestselling books have been written by atheists whose purpose is to deny any existence of God and refute all evidence that proves otherwise. More people are increasingly moving away from truth to satisfy their own desires instead of being bound by rules and regulations that hinder their lifestyles. The phrase "everything is relative" is becoming a dominant force in our society, especially in our schools of higher education. Yet the phrase "everything is relative" refutes itself, in that the statement is asserted as being *true*, which, if so, refutes relativism. No matter how hard we try, we cannot escape truth. But what about God? Is He real? If so, how do we find out?

EVIDENCE OF THE ONE TRUE GOD: THE BIBLE

Our first and greatest evidence of God is the Bible. It was written over a period of 1600 years, by over 40 different authors from various backgrounds. They were fishermen, kings, statesmen, military generals, tax collectors, and others. The Bible was written on three different continents (Asia, Africa and Europe), in three different languages (Hebrew, Aramaic and Greek), with the primary subject being the redemption of man. How could so many authors, living in so many different locations, with multiple generations separating them, write so that their writings would carry the same theme, unless a Divine Being had directed them? The Bible "is the only volume ever produced by man, or a group of men, in which is to be found a large body of prophecies relating to individual nations, to Israel, to all the peoples of the earth, to certain cities, and to the coming of One who was to be the Messiah. The ancient world had many different devices for determining the future, known as divination, but not in the entire gamut of Greek and Latin literature, even though they use the words *prophet* and *prophecy*, can we find any real specific prophecy of a great historic event to come in the distant future, nor any prophecy of a Savior to arise in the human race...."1 "Mohammedanism cannot point to any prophecies of the coming of Mohammed uttered hundreds of years before his birth. Neither can the founders of any cult...rightly identify any ancient text specifically foretelling their appearance."2 The Bible is the only book that fits that category.

Psalm 90:2 says, *"Before the mountains were brought forth, or ever thou hadst formed the earth and the world, even from everlasting to everlasting, thou art God."* Genesis 1:1 says, *"In the beginning God created the heavens and the earth."* These two Bible Scriptures tell us two things: one, God is eternal; and two, He created everything that exists or has existed. Genesis opens with the affirmation of God's existence. He existed before creation, all things were created by Him, and He is before all time. He is eternal!

ETERNAL
Webster's Dictionary defines eternal as "without beginning or end; existing through all time; everlasting." He is without succession or change. "We can say of a creature that it was, is, or will be, but God is! He isn't any more now than He was, and He won't be any more tomorrow than He is today. He is the Eternal 'I Am.' Exodus 3:14. He is of Himself. There is nothing

before Him to cause Him to be. His divine nature is immutable (unchangeable). He is necessarily: a necessity (essential). He has to be what He is. His eternalness is unceasing. He is the same yesterday, today, and forever."3

CREATOR

As Creator, God has life in Himself. "He is, and has life by His essence: that in His being which underlies all outward manifestations and is permanent and unchangeable. God is the originator of all created things. He gives life and light to all things yet receives neither from anything. He who has life within Himself could never be made to exist. If so, life would not be in Him but in whatever made Him exist. Everything depends on Him: He depends on nothing or no one. Before Creation there was only God. All that has ever existed, is, or will exist, was in Him; birthed in Him, made visible by Him."4 The Bible says in Colossians 1:16-17:"*For by him were all things created, that are in heaven and that are in earth, visible and invisible, whether they be thrones or dominions, or principalities, or powers: all things were created by him, and for him: and he is before all things, and by him all things consist.*" Yet, there are those who say they do not believe the Bible and insist there is no God. But are these statements true? What if there is a God? Is there other evidence that He does exist?

THE LAW OF CAUSALITY

To further prove God's existence, let us look at what is called The *Law of Causality*. The *Law of Causality* is a basic principle of science that says that anything that had a beginning also had a cause. There is a cause and effect for everything created. In other words, something—or someone—had to cause things to come into existence. Things cannot come into existence out of nothing. To make a coat, you have to have a coat maker. To make a watch, you have to have a watch maker. Creation did not come into existence by itself. It had to have a *First Cause*, something or someone to create the universe and all that is in it. That *First Cause* is God. Nothing or no one created Him. He has existed for all eternity, with no beginning and no ending. As I said earlier, "He is of Himself." "To deny the *Law of Causality* is to deny rationality. The very process of rational thinking requires us to put together thoughts (the causes) that result in conclusion's (the effects). So if anyone ever tells you he doesn't believe in the *Law of Causality*, simply ask that person, "What caused you to come to that conclusion?" The *Law of Causality* does not say that everything has to have a cause, but everything that comes into being has to have a cause...No one made God...He is an eternal being."5 As the *First Cause*, God brought everything into being by the Word of His power.

Over the centuries, scientists have been doing their best to disprove the existence of God, but they keep running up against a stone wall. In Josh McDowell's book *Evidence That Demands a Verdict*, he states there are three reasons people say there is no God. One is ignorance; two is they want to live in sin and control their own destiny; and three is they do not want to believe, regardless of solid evidence to the contrary. The Bible says in Psalm 14:1, *"The fool hath said in his heart, 'There is no God'."* The Bible also says in Job 12:10 that in God's hand *"...is the life of every living thing, and the breath of all mankind."* In Job 14, verses one and five, it says, *"Man that is born of woman is of few days, and full of trouble...Seeing his days are determined, the number of his months are with thee, thou hast appointed his bounds that he cannot pass."* God controls man's destiny and his time on earth, not man. What people try to do or say to deny the existence of God does not change the fact that He is and that He is eternal. Man is born, lives, and dies; but God continues to live on and perform His good pleasure.

THE FOOLISHNESS OF ATHEISM

"A suggestive scene took place lately in a railway car that was crossing the Rocky Mountains. A quiet business man, who with the other passengers, had been silently watching the vast range of snow-clad peaks, by him seen for the first time, said to his companion: 'No man, it seems to me, could look at that scene without feeling himself brought nearer to his Creator.' A dapper lad of eighteen, who had been chiefly engaged in caressing his mustache, pertly interrupted, 'If you are sure there is a Creator.' 'You are an atheist,' said the stranger, turning to the lad. 'I am an agnostic,' raising his voice. 'I am investigating the subject. I take nothing for granted. I am waiting to be convinced. I see the mountains, I smell the roses, I hear the wind; therefore, I believe that mountains, roses, and wind exist. But I cannot see, smell, or hear God. Therefore—' A grizzled old cattle-raiser glanced over his spectacles at the boy. 'Did you ever try to smell with your eyes?' he said, quietly. 'No.' 'Or hear with your tongue, or taste with your ears?' 'Certainly not.' 'Then why do you try to apprehend God with faculties which are only meant for material things?' 'With what should I apprehend Him?' said the youth, with a conceited giggle. 'With your intellect and soul?—but I beg your pardon'—here he paused—'some men have not breadth and depth enough of intellect and soul to do this. This is probably the reason that you are an agnostic!' The laughter in the car effectually stopped the display of any more atheism that day. (T.Carlyle)"6 It is pure folly to not believe in God. As Norman Geisler says, "I don't have enough faith to be an atheist."

EVOLUTION VS CREATIONISM
When we look at the evolutionary viewpoint of natural selection (the theory that everything evolved from chemicals, or a one-celled amoeba), it seems inconceivable to even consider such a thing, especially when we look at the cellular structure, blood system, and DNA of man. To think that everything came together from a one-celled amoeba without any intelligent intervention is a dead-end street. It took an intelligent being to create that one cell and any chemicals. Something cannot be made out of nothing. Do nonliving chemicals have intelligence? I do not think so. No test tube chemical components have ever produced life. This is the problem with the Darwinists; they cannot explain the origin of the *first* life.

The Bible says that the God of Abraham, Isaac, and Jacob is the Author of life, *"For in him we live, and move, and have our being."* (Acts 17:28 KJV) In Job 12:10, speaking of God, it says, *"In whose hand is the soul of every living thing, and the breath of all mankind."* I do not have enough faith to believe that a one-celled amoeba, or some chemicals, brought forth giant redwood trees, mountains, oceans, rivers, planets, sun, moon, stars, every form of animal life, insect, bird and fish, while at the same time deciding to make human beings with the Moral Law of right and wrong written on their hearts, with a capacity to make choices, and a desire to worship something outside of

"Darwinism asserts that only materials exist, but materials don't have morality. How much does hate weigh? Is there an atom for love? These questions are meaningless because physical particles are not responsible for morality. If materials are solely responsible for morality then Hitler had no real moral responsibility for what he did—he just had bad molecules."8 No, morality is not a physical thing but part of our spiritual makeup from God. We as human beings do not determine what is right and wrong; it is discovered through our conscience. Atheists try to use the aspect of human suffering as proof that there is no God because, they say, if there was a God, He would not allow suffering to continue. But their theory is disproved by the Moral Law (knowing the difference between right and wrong). Since there is a Moral Law, there has to be a Moral Law Giver. We can choose one or the other, but the Moral Law does not change. It is set. Neither atheists nor Darwinists can get away from this, no matter how hard they try.

THE LAWS OF NON-CONTRADICTION AND THE EXCLUDED MIDDLE

This brings us to the laws of Non-Contradiction and the Excluded Middle. The Law of Non-Contradiction and the Excluded Middle are two of the basic laws in classical logic. The law of Non-Contradiction states that "...something cannot be true and not true at the same time when dealing with the same context."9 In other words, a dog cannot be a dog and *not* be a dog at the same time, or a car cannot be a car and *not* be a car at the same time.

The Law of Excluded Middle says, "Statements are either true or false. Or, as some have put it, 'A statement is true or its negation is true.' Some reject this law and assert that there is a third option; namely, that the truth or falsity of the statement can be unknown. But, it would seem that being unknown does not negate the proposition that the statement is either true or false. It just means its truth or falseness is not known."10 So, using these two laws of classic logic, we can say that God is, or God is not; there is no middle ground. When we put all the evidence together, we find that it took an Intelligent Designer to create this universe and everything in it. That Intelligent Designer is God.

CREATURE WORSHIP
It is interesting how man has exchanged his worship of the One True God for the worship of creation. For example, there are people who worship cattle, as well as thousands of gods which men have made with their own hands: gods of wood, gold, silver, bronze, and other idols that cannot see, hear or speak. This idol worship is prevalent in different parts of the world. The Bible speaks of men worshipping created things instead of God in Romans 1:18-25:

"For the wrath of God is revealed from heaven against all ungodliness and unrighteousness of men, who hold the truth in unrighteousness; because that which may be known of God is manifest in them; for God hath shewed it unto them. For the invisible things of him from the creation of the world are clearly seen, being understood by the things that are made, even his eternal power and Godhead; so that they are without excuse: Because that, when they knew God, they glorified him not as God neither were thankful; but became vain in their

imaginations and their foolish heart was darkened. Professing themselves to be wise, they became fools, and changed the glory of the uncorruptible God into an image made like to corruptible man, and to birds, and fourfooted beasts, and creeping things. Wherefore God also gave them up to uncleanness through the lust of their own hearts, to dishonour their own bodies between themselves: who changed the truth of God into a lie, and worshipped and served the creature more than the Creator, who is blessed forever. Amen." (KJV)

A major example of man's worship of creation instead of God is the current Higgs Boson project. In 1964, a physicist by the name of Peter Higgs, along with two other teams, proposed that a subatomic particle, called a *boson*, was the foundational building block of all creation; if found, it would answer the question of how the universe was created, thus proving the evolutionary theory that there is no God who created everything. This unknown boson was later named the "God particle" by Leon Lederman, Director Emeritus of Fermi National Accelerator Laboratory. On the Wikipedia Website, under Higgs Boson, it says, "The Higgs boson or Higgs particle is an elementary particle whose possible discovery was announced on July 4, 2012. It was predicted by a theory in physics called the Standard Model. It is one of the 17 fundamental particles in the Standard Model. The other 16 are the 6 quarks, 6 leptons, the photon, gluon, W, and Z. The quarks and leptons are examples of a class of particles called fermions. They are the ones that make up all the everyday matter we see around us. The photon, W, Z, gluon, and Higgs particles are in a different class called bosons. They are the ones responsible for all the forces in nature except gravity."[11] This is interesting because scientists do not yet know how to combine gravity with the Standard Model.

On the border between France and Switzerland is a machine called the "Large Hadron Collider." It is 328 feet below the ground and is 16.8 miles around. It sends beams of protons and ions around the collider that approach the speed of light. This causes the particles to collide with each other in hopes of revealing the Higgs Boson, or "God particle." Ironically, it was named the "God particle" as an insult to the existence of God. In other words, finding the Higgs Boson, if they do, will disprove God's existence to them. But there are a couple of things wrong here. First and foremost, if they do find this boson, where did it come from? Something cannot come out of nothing, not even a boson. Something or someone had to create it. Second, it brings us back to a basic principle of science: there has to be a *First Cause*, which is God. The boson did not create the boson.

Another problem the scientists have, by their own admission, is that they do not know how to combine gravity with their Standard Model (what the scientists call the twelve building blocks of the universe). Gravity is an unseen force and could not have been created by a boson. This takes us back to the aspect of man rejecting God and worshipping the created amoeba, atoms, and chemicals evolutionists claim created everything. Man wants to be his own god, so he makes up his own rules to live a lifestyle that he desires without any restrictions, or without having to answer to a holy God that created him. But how did all of this come about? Why does man reject the truth of a Divine Being (God) as the Creator of the Universe and all that is in it? The answer will be found in the next chapter and will begin to give us an understanding of the blood and DNA and why God chose blood to redeem not only fallen man, but His entire creation.

THE DISCOVERY OF DNA

In 1869, a Swiss physician and biologist named Johannes Friedrich Miescher was the first researcher to identify DNA (nucleic acids), now known as deoxyribonucleic acid. According to *Webster's Dictionary*, DNA (deoxyribonucleic acid) is "...an essential component of all living matter and a basic material in the chromosomes of the cell nucleus: it contains the genetic code and transmits the hereditary pattern."

It is my understanding that our genes create our chromosomes. There are 46 sets of chromosomes in the human body, arranged in 23 pairs, representing sections of data received from our parents. Each parent contributes one chromosome which combine in the embryo to make a set. Therefore, our genetic message comes equally from each parent. It all has to do with the blood, and this is where the blood of Jesus Christ and His DNA comes into the story. How did God the Son, Jesus Christ, become a man without being conceived through sexual intercourse between a Jewish man and woman and without their DNA being passed on to Him? To find out, we will begin before time, when there was only God, and using history, science, medicine, and the Bible, carry the story forward to the birth of Jesus Christ, His death, Resurrection, ascension to heaven, and His return to rule over the earth out of Jerusalem, Israel.

CHAPTER 2
THE ORIGIN OF SIN AND EVIL

"And there was war in heaven... And the great dragon was cast out, that old serpent, called the devil and satan which deceiveth the whole world: he was cast out into the earth, and his angels were cast out with him." Revelation 12:7-9

In 1981, a Jewish rabbi named Harold Kushner wrote a book called *When Bad Things Happen to Good People*. In the book he tries to explain why an all-powerful, loving God allows sickness, pain, death, and evil things to happen to good people. It is a question that has haunted the minds of men for centuries. The theological term is *Theodicy*: the justice of God in the light of human suffering. If God is perfect, and perfectly holy, then where did evil, sin, sickness, and other infirmities come from? And if He is all-powerful, why does He not put a stop to it? To find out, we have to begin before Creation, when there was only God.

ANGELIC CREATION
Before God created the earth, sun, moon, stars, and our universe, He created angelic beings. How do we know this? In Job 38:1-7, God is speaking to Job about the earth's creation:

"Then the LORD answered Job out of the whirlwind, and said, who is this that darkeneth counsel by words without knowledge? Gird up now thy loins like a man; for I will demand of thee, and answer thou me. Where wast thou when I laid the foundations of the earth declare, if thou hast understanding. Who hath laid the measures thereof if thou knowest? or who hath stretched the line upon it? Whereupon are the foundations thereof fastened? or who laid the corner stone thereof; when the morning stars sang together, and all the sons of God shouted for joy?" (KJV)

In these verses God tells Job that when He created the earth, the angels were there and "shouted for joy." The "sons of God" in the above Scripture is referring to angels (see also Genesis 6:1-2 and Job 1:6).

Unlike man, angels were created individually, with minds of greater capacity than humans and with *free wills*, giving them the power of choice in making decisions; they were to be involved in God's governmental administration over creation, protecting His holiness, and assisting Him as ministering spirits, thus helping fulfill God's plans and purposes for humanity. Hebrews 1:13-14 says, *"But to which of the angels said he at any time, Sit on my right hand, until I make thine enemies thy footstool. Are they not all ministering spirits, sent forth to minister for them who shall be heirs of salvation?"* Angels are immortal and invisible servants and agents of God (although they can appear in human form), and they far exceed humans in power and knowledge. When God created angels, He created different types, classes, and ranks, one of which was the cherubim. They were protectors of God's holiness around His throne, and represented His inflexible righteousness. Since angels were created by God, they knew beyond a doubt that He was the only true God; therefore, if they rebelled against Him, there would be no plan of redemption for them as there would later be for man. This leads us to the origination, and reason, for all the sin and evil that would be brought into the universe.

A HEAVENLY WAR

After God created the angels, everything was perfect in His creation, with total peace and harmony; then something happened to change that. One of God's highest order of angels, a cherub, rebelled against Him and tried to overthrow His kingdom. The angel's name was Lucifer, also called Satan or the Devil. According to Ezekiel 28:14, Satan was a cherub. Although Ezekiel chapter 28 refers to the King of Tyre and the tremendous wealth and commerce he had, verses 13 through 18 are also describing a superhuman being, namely Satan, who was the driving force behind the King of Tyre. The city of Tyre was representative of Satan's commercial system on earth, not only concerning its wealth and commerce but its pride in who it was, as well as its aloofness toward God, Jerusalem, and God's people, the Jews. God ultimately destroyed Tyre because of this. Let us look at the Scriptures regarding Satan:

"You were in Eden (not Adam and Eve's Eden, for the earth had not yet been created), the garden of God; every precious stone was your covering...You were the anointed cherub who covers: I established you; you were on the holy mountain of God...You were perfect in your ways from the day you were created, till iniquity was found in you. By the abundance of your trading you became filled with violence within, and you sinned; therefore I cast you as a profane thing out of

the mountain of God; and I destroyed you, O covering cherub, from the midst of the fiery stones. Your heart was lifted up because of your beauty; you corrupted your wisdom for the sake of your splendor... You defiled your sanctuaries by the multitude of your iniquities, by the iniquity of your trading." (Ezekiel 28:12-18 NKJ)

According to the Scriptures, sin and evil began with this cherub called Satan. He was as close to God, and God's holiness, as anyone could be. In the above scripture, Satan is called the "covering cherub." He was given the awesome privilege and responsibility of serving before, and covering God's throne in heaven. When God gave Moses the design for the Tabernacle in the wilderness, He also gave him the design for the Ark of the Covenant, with the cherubim covering the Mercy Seat as representative of His throne in heaven. According to Hebrews 8:5, it was an "example and shadow of heavenly things." The Ark was placed in the "Most Holy Place" in the Tabernacle in the wilderness, as well as in the Temple in Jerusalem that King Solomon built. Exodus 25:10,17-22 says:

"And they shall make an ark of shittim wood...And thou shalt make a mercy seat of pure gold... And thou shalt make two cherubim of gold, of beaten work shalt thou make them, in the two ends of the mercy seat...And the cherubim shall stretch forth their wings on high, covering the mercy seat with their wings, and their faces shall look one to another; toward the mercy seat shall the faces of the cherubim be. And thou shalt put the mercy seat above upon the ark; and in the ark thou shalt put the testimony that I shall give thee. And there I will meet with thee, and I will commune with thee from above the mercy seat, from between the two cherubim which are upon the ark of

the testimony, of all things which I will give thee in commandment unto the children of Israel." (KJV)

As God gave commands and instructions to His angels from His heavenly throne, so would He do the same with Moses on earth from above the Mercy Seat in the tabernacle in the wilderness, after Israel's deliverance from Egypt and before they entered the land of Canaan.

Second, God created Satan as a perfect being with tremendous power and position in God's kingdom; but his beauty, talent, and giftings, along with the commerce God had entrusted to him, caused him to become self-exalted, and he sinned. He "corrupted his wisdom for the sake of his splendor." In other words, the pride of who he was is what brought him down. He became jealous of God and God's position, as we will see in Isaiah 14:12-15. He thought he could take over God's throne and become ruler of all of God's creation. So, all sin and evil originated from Satan. As the anointed cherub, he went from being holy to being filled with all iniquity. Having a free will, Satan's sin was *self-born*. He became self-occupied with his own beauty, power, and accomplishments; he turned from his dependence upon God to self-dependence. He became the personification of evil: from lust and greed to hatred, vanity, envy, destruction, and every other thing that is opposed to God's love, righteousness, holiness, and justice. He changed his position from that of a holy cherub to that of becoming the father of all lies, sin, and evil. He became Satan, the slanderer and adversary of God, as well as the accuser and destroyer of much of the human race that God would later create.

Isaiah 14:1-23 addresses the King of Babylon. The Jewish prophet Isaiah tells us that Babylon was emerging as a world power (through war) and was acquiring wealth and power from the nations around them, as well as killing and enslaving the people. As in Ezekiel 28:13-18, there is a dual meaning behind verses twelve through fifteen. They describe Satan, who is Lucifer, as that superhuman being who was also the driving force behind the King of Babylon, as he was with the King of Tyre:

"How art thou fallen from heaven, O Lucifer, son of the morning! how art thou cut down to the ground, which didst weaken the nations! For thou hast said in thine heart, I will ascend into heaven, I will exalt my throne above the stars of God: I will sit also upon the mount of the congregation, in the sides of the north: I will ascend above the heights of the clouds; I will be like the most High." (Isaiah 14:12-15 KJV)

As Ezekiel 28 was representative of Satan's commercial system on earth, so Babylon was representative of his religious system. As stated before, Satan was not satisfied with his position in God's creation. He wanted to take over God's throne and kingdom, so he conceived a plan of rebellion and war against God, drawing a third of the angels of heaven with him. We see this satanic nature playing out today in every area of society, as men and women grapple for position, money, and power using the same tactics Satan used in trying to overthrow God's kingdom. (Satan uses systematic methods to accomplish his purposes.) Jealousy, pride, deceit, lying, and rebellion rule in the hearts and minds of unregenerate men and women--from our homes to our learning institutions to the governments of the world, as they reject and usurp God's position in their lives and set themselves up as their own gods on the thrones of their hearts.

HEAVEN'S HALLS STAINED

Have you ever thought about the movies that have been made where the bad guys try to overthrow the good king and his kingdom; then, when it seems that all is lost and the bad guys are going to win, the good king rides in on his white horse with major reinforcements, defeats the bad guys, and saves his kingdom? What about real wars, such as World War II, when the enemy, namely Hitler and the German army, tried to conquer not only the nations around him but the world? In both cases, in the movies or on the real battlefield, much blood was shed for the sake of freedom. So it was in heaven as the devil and his angels tried to overthrow God and His kingdom. There was major warfare and, according to the Scriptures, blood was shed as angels fought against angels. In the aftermath of this war, due to Satan's rebellion, heaven was stained with sin and God would need something or someone to cleanse it. That Someone would be Jesus Christ and His pure, sinless blood. Hebrews 9:22-24 is a scripture which validates this:

"And almost all things are by the law purged with blood, and without shedding of blood is no remission. It was therefore necessary that the patterns of things in the heavens should be purified with these; but the <u>"heavenly things"</u> themselves <u>"with better sacrifices"</u> than these. For Christ is not entered into the holy places made with hands, which are the figures of the true; but into heaven itself, now to appear in the presence of God for us." (KJV. Emphasis mine.)

Just as the earthly tabernacle and Temple had to be purified with the blood of animals, so did heaven have to be purified with blood--not the blood of animals but the pure, sinless blood of Jesus Christ. Some would say that angels are spirit beings and could not possibly have blood; nor could blood have been shed in heaven when Satan and the angels that followed him made war against God. But is that true? Is there any more evidence to give credence to our exegesis? Yes. The Bible is very clear that angels can take on human form, as in the case of the three angels, one of which was the LORD (the pre-incarnate Christ), who came to Abraham and had a meal with him in Genesis, chapter 18. Also, Hebrews 13:2 says, *"Be not forgetful to entertain strangers, for thereby some have entertained angels unawares."* (KJV)

ANGELS AND DNA

Genesis, chapter 6, is really interesting regarding angels and DNA and seems to bring more validation to blood being a part of their makeup:

"And it came to pass, when men began to multiply on the face of the earth, and daughters were born unto them, that the sons of God saw the daughters of men that they were fair; and they took them wives of all which they chose. And the LORD said, My spirit shall not always strive with man, for that he also is flesh; yet his days shall be an hundred and twenty years. There were giants in the earth in those days and also after that, when the sons of god came in unto the daughters of men, and they bear children to them, the same became mighty men which were of old, men of renown." (Genesis 6:1-4 KJV)

Some Bible scholars have stated that the "sons of god" in these scriptures represent the godly seed of the Sethites marrying the ungodly seed of the Cainites, or of kings and nobles marrying commoners; but neither of these theories fits the context, nor do they explain how such unions could bring forth giants, leading to such violence and corruption upon the earth that God would destroy all of humanity (except Noah and his family) with a flood. "Neither the descendants of Seth nor true believers of any sort have been previously referred to in Genesis as sons of God in any kind of spiritual sense and, except for Adam himself, they could not have been sons of God in a physical sense....These beings were sons of God, rather than of men, because they had been created, not born. Such a description, of course, would apply only to Adam (Luke 3:38) and to the angels, whom God had directly created (Psalm 148:2, 5; Psalm 104:4; Colossians 1:16). The actual phrase *bene elohim* is used three other times, all in the very ancient book of Job (1:6; 2:1; 38:7). There is no doubt at all that, in these passages, the meaning applies exclusively to the angels. A very similar form (*bar elohim*) is used in Daniel 3:25, and also refers either to an angel or to a theophany...Thus, there seems no reasonable doubt that, in so far as the language itself is concerned, the intent of the writer was to convey the thought of angels—fallen angels, no doubt, since they were acting in opposition to God's will. This also was the meaning placed on the passage by the Greek translators of the Septuagint, by Josephus, by the writer of the ancient apocryphal book of Enoch, and by all the other ancient Jewish interpreters and the earliest Christian writers.

It is true that the Lord Jesus said that *"in the resurrection they neither marry nor are given in marriage, but are as the angels of God in heaven"* (Matthew 22:30). However, this is not equivalent to saying that angels are "sexless", since people who share in the resurrection will surely retain their own personal identity, whether male or female."1 If these fallen angels cohabited with the daughters of men and birthed children, as the Scripture says, then the angels would have had to have blood in their beings, and their DNA would have been passed on to their children, thus birthing a perverted race on the earth. This would make more sense of Jude verse 6: *"And the angels which kept not their first estate, but left their own habitation, he hath reserved in everlasting chains under darkness unto the judgment of the great day."* And, II Peter 2:4: *"For if God spared not the angels that sinned, but cast them down to hell, and delivered them into chains of darkness to be reserved unto judgment...."* This brings us to the conclusion that Satan, through the fallen angels cohabiting with the daughters of men, was trying to corrupt and destroy Adam and Eve's progeny that would bring forth the promised Seed who would defeat Satan forever. Again, it goes back to the blood. We will cover this in more detail later.

ANGELIC SWORDS
Another question we must answer is why do angels have swords if not for battle? Genesis 3:23 tells us when God drove Adam and Eve out of the Garden of Eden, He *"placed at the east of the garden of Eden Cherubims, and a flaming sword which turned every way, to keep the way of the tree of life."* In Numbers 22:23, 31-33, an angel of the LORD stands in the path of the soothsayer Balaam and his donkey, with a sword in his hand, ready to kill Balaam. The donkey sees the angel but Balaam does not, so he

strikes the animal to make it go forward. Then, Balaam's eyes were opened to see the angel also. *"And the ass saw the angel of the LORD standing in the way, and his sword drawn in his hand...then the LORD opened the eyes of Balaam, and he saw the angel of the LORD standing in the way, and his sword drawn in his hand:...And the angel of the LORD said unto him, Wherefore hast thou smitten thine ass these three times: unless she had turned from me, surely now also I had slain thee, and saved her alive."* This shows emphatically that the angel's sword was used as a weapon to kill. Another instance is in Ezekiel, chapter 9, when God sends the six angels to Jerusalem to slay the wicked.

There are three more Scriptures that seem to validate what we have been saying about blood being shed in heaven during Satan's war against God. They are Isaiah 34:5, Revelation 19:11-16, and Isaiah 24:21-23, all of which are referring to end times, the "Day of the Lord" and the return of Jesus Christ to the earth to establish His kingdom rule.

When Jesus returns, He will do battle with, and defeat, the host of the evil spirits of heaven before defeating the armies of the nations. Isaiah 34:5 says, *"For my sword shall be bathed in heaven: behold, it shall come down upon Idumea, and upon the people of my curse, for judgment."* The word *bathed* is a Hebrew prime root word meaning to make drunk, to satiate, or to soak. If we understand this correctly, Jesus' sword will be soaked with the blood of the evil spirits of heaven as He does battle with them upon His return to earth. Revelation 19:11-16 speaks of this also:

"And I saw heaven opened, and behold a white horse; and he that sat upon him was called Faithful and True, and in righteousness he doth judge and make war. His eyes were as a flame of fire, and on his head were many crowns; and he had a name written, that no man knew, but he himself. And **he was clothed with a vesture dipped in blood:** *and his name is called The Word of God. And the armies which were in heaven followed him upon white horses, clothed in fine linen, white and clean. And out of His mouth goeth a sharp sword, that with it he should smite the nations: and he shall rule them with a rod of iron: and he treadeth the winepress of the fierceness and wrath of Almighty God. And he hath on his vesture and on his thigh a name written KING OF KINGS AND LORD OF LORDS."*(KJV. Emphasis mine.)

In the above Scriptures, John sees Jesus Christ returning to earth with His robe dipped in blood.

If we take these verses in sequence, this happens before He deals with the nations; and, as I said before, He will do battle with the fallen angels on His way back to earth and will punish not only the spiritual forces of darkness but also the kings of the earth and put them in prison until the time of their final judgment:

"And it shall come to pass in that day, that the LORD shall punish the host of the high ones that are on high, and the kings of the earth upon the earth. And they shall be gathered together, as prisoners are gathered in the pit, and shall be shut up in the prison, and after many days shall they be visited (punished). Then the moon shall be confounded, and the sun ashamed when the LORD of hosts shall

reign in mount Zion, and in Jerusalem, and before his ancients gloriously." (Isaiah 24:21-24 KJV)

The "host of high the ones that are on high" refers to the fallen angels and demon spirits that have plagued humanity over the centuries.

So why is blood so important? Why did God require blood to cleanse the halls of heaven after Satan's rebellion? Why does Satan hate humanity so much that he has done everything he can to contaminate and destroy the human body and its blood system, if there is not something of great value in the blood and DNA of man? It is interesting that demon powers have a thirst for blood. Israel knew this, and that is why God instructed them not to eat blood but to cover the blood with dust after an animal had been slain:

"For the life of the flesh is in the blood; and I have given it to you upon the altar to make an atonement for your souls: for it is the blood that maketh an atonement for the soul. Therefore I said unto the children of Israel, No soul of you shall eat blood, neither shall any stranger that sojourneth among you eat blood. And whatsoever man there be of the children of Israel or of the strangers that sojourn among you, which hunteth and catcheth any beast or fowl that may be eaten; he shall even pour out the blood thereof, and cover it with dust." (Leviticus 17:11-13 KJV)

BLOOD: THE FOOD OF DEMONS

Before Israel entered the land of Canaan, God warned them not to partake of the evil of the Canaanites or their idolatrous rituals. The Canaanites worshipped and served Baal, which means, lord, possessor, husband, master, owner. We know what cannibalism *is*, but what does it really mean? It is a blood covenant word which comes from Canaan and Baal, and it has to do with eating human sacrifices. Cannibalism is a covenant meal at Satan's table, the counterfeit to God's Table of Communion. Human flesh and blood was the most valued sacrifice and most accepted by the gods (demons and Satan). The people believed the sacrifice became the food of the god to whom they offered it; thus the offerer ate it for nourishment and growth which resulted in life, the life of that god. The blood was poured out on the ground or altar and was the food of the demons. Clay Trumbull, in his book *The Blood Covenant*, says, "Among all nations, from the beginning, sacrifice has been a means of seeking union with God or gods. It has always been known to be a possibility." Here are some examples:

Mamonides, the great Jewish rabbi says "the Sabeans partook of blood because they thought it was the food of the spirits; by eating it man has something in common with the spirits, which join him and tell him future events, according to the notions which people generally have of spirits. Other peoples killed the sacrifice and ate of its flesh while catching the blood in a pot and sitting around it waiting for the spirits to come partake of the blood which was their food. While eating together they came into brotherhood and established friendships. The spirits telling them of future events and being favorable to them. (3 *Guide of the Perplexed*, Friedlander's Translation, III. 232)."2

Rabbi Moses bar Nachman says "the ancient heathens in their worship of their idol gods" gathered together blood for the devils their idol gods, and then came themselves and did eat of

28

that blood with them as the devils' guests, invited to eat at the table of devils. Thus they were joined in federal society with them. *(Intellectual System of the Universe,* Andover ed., *H., 542).*"3

St. Basil says, "Sacrifices are things of no small pleasure and advantage to demons; because the blood, being evaporated by fire, is taken into the compages [framework] and substances of their bodies; the whole of which [bodily substance] is throughout nourished with vapors. *(Intellectual System of the Universe: Commentary on Isaiah,* Harrison Cudworth)."4

This, according to Trumbull, prevailed among the Greeks and Romans, and even many of the Christian fathers accepted its truth as applicable to the demons. (Citations from *Porphyry and Origen, Harrison Cudworth's Intellectual System of the Universe, with Mosheim's notes.* III.,350-352.)5

It is no small wonder that blood plays such an important part in Satan's kingdom or that demons relish the blood, as it is their food. These spirits also use human spirits to fulfill their lust for blood by inhabiting them and causing a desire in the person or tribe to drink blood. This is worshipping Satan at his table of inter-union and inter-communion. It is the counterfeit for God's Table of Communion known as The Lord's Supper.

All the Scriptures and references used in this chapter confirm where sin and evil originated and that God did not create evil. It was inborn in Satan who was created with a free will to choose. But God had a plan to bring total restoration of peace and harmony back to His creation that was disrupted by

Satan's rebellion. It would take seven thousand years to fulfill, but it would be accomplished.

Chapter 3
A LEVEL PLAYING FIELD

"In the beginning God created the heavens and the earth."
(Genesis 1:1)

No one knows the time span between Satan's rebellion against God and God's creation of the heavens and earth. What we do know is that Satan's rebellion had a massive affect on God's kingdom. Evidently, as Satan looked around him at what he had and who he was, he felt that he was strong enough, wise enough, and able to muster enough support to overthrow God or he never would have tried. Because of Satan's rebellion, God could have immediately destroyed him and his followers, since He was their Creator, but He did not. Why? He had an infallible plan to deal with Satan and his emissaries on a level playing field that would ultimately defeat them, confine them to an eternal place of fire and brimstone, and restore order, peace, harmony, and authority back to His creation. It would be a progressive plan that would include the creation of the sun, moon, stars, the earth, and man, and it would rid God's universe of sin and evil forever. This plan of redemption would first be revealed in the stars and then be played out on earth, beginning in the Middle East.

SIGNS IN THE HEAVENS
Behind every major building project there is a set of blueprints, drawn up by an architect, showing every detail of what is to be built, along with a scale model of what the finished product

will look like. This is so even with God, the Designer and Maker of all. On the fourth day of Creation He created the sun, moon, and stars, and in the stars he placed an architectural drawing of His plan of redemption that would be revealed to astronomers down through the centuries, as well as a sign to humanity that He was the Creator of the Universe (see Psalm 19). This redemption plan, written in the heavens, would be implemented in actuality by Adam and Eve, the man and woman He would later create on earth on the sixth day.

Due to the vast amount of subject matter regarding man's redemption written in the stars, I am only going to touch on it, showing that blood and DNA is represented, in type, in the Signs of the Zodiac and the story they tell. For example, "Virgo is represented as a woman with a *branch* in her right hand, and some ears of corn in her left hand, thus giving a twofold testimony of the Coming One. The name of this sign in the Hebrew is *Betulah* which means *a virgin*, and in the Arabic a *branch*. The two words are connected, as in Latin—*Virgo*, which means *a virgin*; and *virga*, which means *a branch* (Vulg. Isa, xi, 1). The sign of the virgin is referred to in Isaiah 7:14 regarding a coming Jewish Messiah, Jesus Christ, who would be born of a virgin. *Behold, a virgin shall conceive and bear a son, and shall call his name Immanuel.*"[1] "The brightest star in Virgo has an ancient name, handed down to us in all the star-maps, in which the Hebrew word *Tsemech is preserved.* It is called in Arabic *Al Zimach*, which means *the branch*. Once again, this refers to a coming Messiah who will be called *The Branch.*"[2]

"Behold, the days come, saith the LORD, that I will raise unto David a righteous BRANCH. And a KING shall reign and prosper." (Jeremiah 23:5-6 KJV)

Virgo and other signs of the constellations—such as the Serpent, the Dragon and the Scorpion (all types of Satan), the Bear, the Water Bearer, Leo the lion, and others—depict different aspects of creation, their DNA, and God's plan of redemption that would be fulfilled on earth in a very unusual and miraculous way. (Google "Gospel of the Stars.") Also, Psalm 19:1-4 speaks of this.

SATAN'S DEATH KNELL
As stated earlier in this book, God could have immediately destroyed Satan when he rebelled, but He did not. Because Heaven was stained with sin, that stain had to be removed; and the only way to do that was with blood. Satan neither knew nor understood this plan until it was too late. God would take the battle to earth and deal with Satan in a way that all of creation would see His power, wisdom, and glory. God's plan of redemption would now begin to be implemented through His highest creation, man and woman: their bloodlines, DNA, and the promise of a Coming Redeemer.

THE FORBIDDEN FRUIT
The scene begins after God creates Adam and Eve and places them in The Garden of Eden, in a country known today as Iraq. (Adam and Eve, our first ancestors, did not originate from Africa, as has been propagated.) There Adam is instructed by God to tend the Garden. In the garden were two specific trees: the Tree of Life and the Tree of the Knowledge of Good and

Evil. God gave Adam and his wife, Eve, freedom to eat of every tree of the garden *except* the Tree of the Knowledge of Good and Evil. If they ate of its fruit, they would surely die, both physically (over time) and spiritually (by being separated from God for violating His Word).

"And the LORD God took the man, and put him into the garden of Eden to dress it and to keep it. And the LORD God commanded the man, saying, Of every tree of the garden thou mayest freely eat. But of the tree of the knowledge of good and evil, thou shalt not eat of it: for in the day that thou eatest thereof thou shalt surely die." (Genesis 2:15-17 KJV)

According to the Scriptures, the Serpent (Satan) tempted Eve to eat of the forbidden fruit:

"Now the serpent was more subtle than any beast of the field which the LORD God had made. And he said unto the woman Yea, hath God said, Ye shall not eat of every tree of the garden? And the woman said unto the serpent, We may eat of the fruit of the trees of the garden: But of the fruit of the tree which is in the midst of the garden, God hath said, Ye shall not eat of it neither shall ye touch it, lest ye die. And the serpent said unto the woman, Ye shall not surely die: For God doth know that in the day ye eat thereof, then your eyes shall be opened, and ye shall be as gods, knowing good and evil." (Genesis 3:1-5 KJV)

Why was Satan so intent on Eve's eating the forbidden fruit? What was his motive? First, he wanted them to *go against God*; second, he wanted *to get to their blood systems*. Satan knew there was something about eating of the fruit of the tree that would cause them, not only to violate God's Word, but cause their deaths. Adam had been created in the image of God and Eve was created from one of Adam's ribs. They were both perfect and reflections of God's glory on earth, which caused Satan to despise them. The Tree of the Knowledge of Good and Evil was their test in keeping God's Word, but Satan used the same tactics on Eve that caused his demise, in that he had not been satisfied with what God had given him; he wanted it all. Now he tempted Eve to take possession of the only tree in the garden that was off limits to her and Adam by appealing to her senses.

*"And **when the woman saw** that the tree was **good for food,** and that it was **pleasant to the eyes,** and **a tree to be desired to make one wise,** she took of the fruit thereof, and did eat, and gave also unto her husband with her; and he did eat. And the eyes of them both were opened, and they knew they were naked; and they sewed fig leaves together, and made themselves aprons."* (Genesis 3:6-7 KJV. Emphasis mine.)

Satan had succeeded in his mission and probably thought the human race would now be his confederates and servants forever, but two things happened that he did not count on. First, the Tree of the Knowledge of Good and Evil was placed in the Garden of Eden by God to trap Satan and eventually seal his doom. Second, Adam's and Eve's eating of the forbidden fruit was Satan's death knell, the catalyst that began the process of redemption for all of creation. Did God know beforehand that Adam and Eve would violate His Word and eat of the tree? Yes. How do we know? The Scriptures tell us of a Coming One (Jesus Christ) who would redeem not only those who would believe in Him, but all of creation.

"Forasmuch as ye know that ye were not redeemed with corruptible things, as silver and gold, from your vain conversation received by tradition from your fathers; but with the precious blood of Christ, as of a lamb without blemish and without spot: **Who verily was foreordained before the foundation of the world**, *but was manifest in these last times for you, who by him do believe in God, that raised him up from the dead, and gave him glory; that your faith and hope might be in God."* (I Peter 1:18-21 KJV. Emphasis mine.)

"Because the creation itself also will be delivered from the bondage of corruption into the glorious liberty of the children of God." (Romans 8:21 NKJV) This was God's plan, and it would be carried out over a period of centuries, culminating in the victory of Jesus Christ, through His shed blood, Crucifixion, death, burial and Resurrection, and His ultimate return to earth to establish His kingdom rule.

CONSEQUENCES OF DISOBEDIENCE
What happened when Adam and Eve ate of the forbidden fruit? First, they violated God's Word, causing a spiritual separation between them and God. Second, there was something in the forbidden fruit that changed their blood chemistry, triggering the death process in their physical bodies and setting in motion the Second Law of Thermodynamics, the Law of Entropy (the deterioration of life). What was in the fruit that caused this to happen? We do not know for sure, but in 2005 I wrote an essay regarding this, sent it to a Congressman friend of mine to read; he, in turn, sent it to a friend of his who

was a Research Immunologist. Upon reading the essay, the immunologist stated that the ingested fruit, having entered Adam's and Eve's blood systems, could possibly have caused a *Retrovirus*, and/or *Oxidative Stress*. Regarding Retrovirus, I knew the meaning of *retro*, which means "back, backwards," but not being a biologist, I looked up the meaning of *virus* in the Oxford Dictionary. The origin of the word *virus* is, guess what...*snake venom*. From Latin, literally "slimy liquid, poison."

The medical meaning of *Retrovirus* is as follows. "Any of several viruses whose genetic specification is encoded in RNA rather than DNA and that are able to reverse the normal flow of genetic information from DNA to RNA by transcribing RNA into DNA."[3] Retroviruses cause different diseases.

Oxidative stress is "physiological stress on the body that is caused by the cumulative damage done by free radicals inadequately neutralized by antioxidants and that is held to be associated with aging."[4]

Not only does the body begin to deteriorate, but Oxidative Stress can cause more than two hundred known diseases. I am not saying this is exactly what happened when Adam and Eve ate of the forbidden fruit, but it is a possibility. Only God knows.

By eating of the forbidden fruit, Adam and Eve were poisoned, not only physically but spiritually, and their spiritual and physical degeneration would be passed on to their progeny; but God would intervene and make a way, through blood, for fallen men and women to come back into fellowship and communion with Him.

Chapter 4
THE PROMISED SEED

"And I will put enmity between you and the woman..."
(Genesis 3:15 NKJ)

Adam and Eve disobeyed God, knew they were naked, and tried to hide from Him in the garden. When God addressed Adam, asking if he had eaten of the forbidden fruit, Adam said "yes" but blamed God for giving him Eve; then he blamed Eve who, in turn, blamed the serpent. Now, instead of being the pure and holy man and woman God had created, their new sin nature took over. Somehow, by disobeying God's Word and eating of the forbidden fruit, the nature of Satan began to be manifested in them. They were now walking in fear; and an evil, accusing spirit was operating in each of them, as Adam accused Eve and Eve accused the serpent of being responsible for their disobedience.

*"And they heard the voice of the LORD God walking in the garden in the cool of the day: and Adam and his wife hid themselves from the presence of the LORD God amongst the trees of the garden. and the LORD God called unto Adam, and said unto him, Where art thou? And he said, **I heard thy voice** in the garden, and **I was afraid**, because **I was naked**; and **I hid myself**. And he said, Who told thee that thou wast naked? Hast thou eaten of the tree, whereof I commanded thee that thou shouldest not eat? And **the man said**, The **woman** whom thou gavest to be with me, **she gave me of the tree**, and I did eat. And the LORD God said unto the woman, What is this*

*that thou hast done? And the **woman said, The serpent beguiled me** and I did eat."* (Genesis 3:8-13 KJV. Emphasis mine.)

This sin nature would continue, passed on through the blood system and DNA, of Adam and Eve to each succeeding generation. No human being ever born would be exempt, except the coming Redeemer, Jesus Christ, by way of a virgin birth. *"Wherefore, as by one man (Adam) sin entered into the world, and death by sin; and so death passed upon all men, for that all have sinned. (Romans 5:12 KJV) (Emphasis mine.) "For all have sinned, and come short of the glory of God."* (Romans 3:23 KJV) Jesus Christ was the only person to ever live who would be sinless, other than Adam and Eve before they sinned. *"...Christ also suffered for us, leaving us an example, that ye should follow his steps: Who did no sin, neither was guile found in his mouth."* (I Peter 2:21-22 KJV) All of humanity is related by blood to Adam and Eve, as the Bible says: *"And hath made of **one blood** all nations of men for to dwell on all the face of the earth..."* (Acts 17:26 KJV) (Emphasis mine.)

A very important point to remember is that Adam's and Eve's flesh was not sinful. It was their minds (their will, intellect, and emotions) that caused them to sin. They yielded to their senses: what they saw, heard, touched, smelled, and tasted. Their bodies were just the instruments to bring it all about. Even little children exhibit this sin nature at a very young age, through meanness, greed, rebellion, sneakiness, temper tantrums, and such. They do not have to be taught these things; it is inborn in the blood and DNA passed down from Adam and Eve.

THE ENMITY

Since God knew beforehand that Adam and Eve would violate His Word and eat of the forbidden fruit, how would He fulfill His plan to bring forth a Redeemer, a Messiah who would defeat Satan and bring restoration to His creation? The Scriptures tell us:

"And I will put enmity between you and the woman, and between your seed and her seed; He shall bruise your head, and You shall bruise his heel." (Genesis 3:15 NKJ)

This scripture is the first to give hope and promise of a Coming Redeemer who would defeat Satan and bring in everlasting righteousness. It is called *the protevangelium,* or *the first gospel.* It is a Messianic Scripture supported by the early Church Fathers, as well as the Jerusalem Targum [Targum: Aramaic paraphrasings and explanatory translations of the Hebrew Scriptures], Targum of Jonathan, and the Mishnah—*the written oral law.* (Sotah 9:15) God tells Satan He will put *enmity* between him and the woman. "The direct object (enmity) stands first in the Hebrew sentence for emphasis. The term is never used in a relation to dumb beasts. The verse, therefore, is not merely a primitive tale designed to speculate about the origin of the dislike most people feel toward reptiles. God is speaking here of hostility—active hatred—between two intelligent beings, satanic Serpent and Eve. It was God himself who placed this enmity in the heart of the woman...Now she recognized Satan as her malevolent enemy who was determined to destroy her. She would need help in battling him in the future, and God promised to give her that help. He would help her hate Satan."1

This *enmity* would be between Satan's *seed* and Eve's *seed*. Both seeds would come from Eve, but Satan's seed would be those human beings who would choose to do the bidding of Satan, while Eve's seed would be the godly line who would do God's bidding and be at enmity with Satan and his forces of evil. Therefore, the term *seed* is used not only in the physical sense but in the spiritual and moral sense, as well. Genesis 3:15 shows us that this personal warfare between Satan and Eve would be carried forward to succeeding generations in the spiritual and moral realm; the followers of God would do battle not just against ungodly men and women under Satan's control but also against the spiritual forces of darkness. Both of these seeds would be passed on through the blood and DNA of their respective seeds.

We must remember also that through God's plan of redemption there would be those, down through the ages, who would defect from Satan's dominion, receive God's forgiveness, be saved, and have God's enmity against Satan put in them in order to live godly lives. It is interesting that everyone who has ever chosen to serve God and make Jesus Christ Lord of their lives had to make that decision through the convicting power of the Holy Spirit, whether through hearing the Word of God preached, through someone's testimony, through reading the Scriptures, or by a personal encounter with Jesus Christ. The Scriptures tell us in II Timothy 2:19:

"Nevertheless the foundation of God standeth sure, having this seal, **The Lord knoweth them that are his.** *And let everyone that nameth the name of Christ depart from iniquity."* (Emphasis mine.)

There will also be those who will choose to become apostates, turning from serving God to following Satan, allowing their fleshly, selfish desires to take over, thus living a life of sin and debauchery. We see this in the Scriptures in II Thessalonians 2:1-3, referring to a *great falling away*, or *apostasy*, of those who forsake their relationship with Jesus Christ and follow Satan in the last days before His return.

*"Now we beseech you, brethren, by the coming of our Lord Jesus Christ, and by our gathering together unto him, that ye be not soon shaken in mind or be troubled neither by spirit, nor by word, nor by letter as from us, as that the day of Christ is at hand. Let no man deceive you by any means: for that day shall not come, except there come a falling away first **(apostasy)**, and that man of sin be revealed, the son of perdition."* (KJV. Emphasis mine.)

This is also expressed in I Timothy 4:1: *"Now the Spirit speaketh expressly, that in the latter times some shall depart from the faith, giving heed to seducing spirits, and doctrines of devils."*

We will begin to see this play out in the next chapter as Satan, working through Cain, the ungodly seed, tries to destroy God's promise of a Coming Redeemer when he murders Abel.

THREE-FOLD ASPECT OF MESSIAH
The last part of Genesis 3:15 *"...He shall bruise your head, and you shall bruise His heel,"* reveals the final outcome of a battle that would take place centuries later as the lineage of the godly seed of Eve would bring forth the Messiah Redeemer who, through His pure, sinless blood, would defeat Satan forever.

"The passage provides a fitting description of Satan's ways. The heel may not represent as crucial a point of attack as the head. But it indicates fittingly the subversiveness of the Deceiver. If the heel may be regarded as the object of subversive attack and partial wound (despite a fatal intention), the head represents the object of open attack and mortal wound. The seed of the woman shall crush the serpent's head. Satan shall be bruised mortally, defeated totally."2

In Genesis 3:15, and later in every division of the Tenach [an acronym for the Law, *Torah*; the Prophets, *Nevi'im*; and the Writings, which are the Psalms, *Kethubim*], we find the three-fold aspect of this *Seed*.

1. The Torah (the first five books of the Bible) tells us *Messiah is a person*:

"The scepter shall not depart from Judah, Nor a lawgiver from between his feet, until Shiloh comes; and to Him shall be the obedience of the people." (Genesis 49:10 NKJ)

*"I will raise up for them a Prophet like you from among their brethren, and will put My words in His mouth, and He shall speak to them all that I command Him. (*Deuteronomy 18:1 NKJ*)*

2. The Prophets tell us *He will suffer* then be raised from the dead as King Messiah:

"He is despised and rejected by men, A Man of sorrows and acquainted with grief. He was oppressed and He was afflicted, Yet He opened not His mouth; He was led as a lamb to the slaughter, And as

a sheep before its shearers is silent, So He opened not his mouth. He was taken from prison and from judgment, And who will declare His generation? For he was cut off from the land of the living; For the transgressions of My people He was stricken. Yet it pleased the Lord to bruise Him; He has put Him to grief. When You make His soul an offering for sin, he shall see His seed, he shall prolong His days, And the pleasure of the Lord shall prosper in His hand. (Isaiah 53:3, 7-8, 10 NKJ)

3. The Writings tell us He will be from the *house and lineage of David*:

"The Lord has sworn in truth to David; he will not turn from it: "I will set upon your throne the fruit of your body." (Psalm 132:11 NKJ)

"The Lord said to my Lord, "Sit at My right hand, Till I make Your enemies Your footstool." (Psalm 110:1 NKJ)

In Psalm 110, King David speaks concerning His Lord Messiah as sitting at the right hand of God. This Messiah, though still God, would come to earth in the form of man, through the lineage of King David. He would encounter enemies while on earth, would ascend to heaven at God's right hand for a season, and then return to put all these enemies under His feet.

When Jesus Christ (*Yeshua* in Hebrew) came to His disciples after His resurrection, He reminded them that He was the One who fulfilled the Messianic prophecies of the Tenach:

"Then He said to them. "These are the words which I spoke to you while I was still with you, that all things must be fulfilled which were written in the Law of Moses and the Prophets and the Psalms concerning Me." And He opened their understanding, that they might comprehend the Scriptures. (Luke 24:44-45 NKJ)

Here the Tenach gives us a most clear picture of the birth, life, death, Resurrection, and reign of Jesus Christ the Messiah, King of Kings, and Lord of the universe. He was the *Seed of the woman who bruised the head of the serpent*!

JEWISH THOUGHT ON GENESIS 3:15
The Midrash, Bereshith Rabba 23 (the rabbinical commentary on the Book of Genesis), explains that in this passage *another seed* means *a seed which comes from another place*. In other words, this other seed was to be the Jewish Messiah who would come from heaven and be born of a virgin supernaturally (Isaiah 7:14; 9:6-7). It refers to the Book of Ruth, chapter 4 verse 18, in explaining this: *"Now this is the genealogy of Perez: Perez begot Hezron.* (NKJ) This scripture shows what family line *the Seed* (Messiah) would come through.

Perez was a son of Judah from whose lineage came King David and from which would come Messiah. It is strange how the Jewish sages pinpointed this scripture as Messianic yet failed to see Jesus Christ (*Yeshua*) as their Messiah, especially since Matthew and Luke trace His genealogy back to Perez.

The Jewish scholars also refer to Psalm 40:7-8: *"Then I said, "Behold, I come; In the scroll of the Book it is written of me. I delight to do Your will, O my God, And Your law is within my heart."* (NKJ)

This scripture foretells the coming of Messiah who would be obedient to God, give His *life*, and usher in the New Covenant in His pure, sinless blood which would free man from sin and death. He would be the perfect sacrifice.

Because of Adam's and Eve's disobedience, God drove them out of the Garden of Eden and placed cherubim with flaming swords at the East of the Garden to keep them out lest they would eat of the Tree of Life and live forever.

God told Eve she would bear children in pain and her grief would be greatly multiplied. As for Adam, God passed a fourfold sentence on him.

"The curse on man himself was fourfold: (1) sorrow, resulting from continual disappointment and futility; (2) pain and suffering, signified by the thorns which intermittently hinder man in his efforts to provide a living for his family; (3) sweat, or tears, the strong crying of intense struggle against a hostile environment; and finally (4) physical death, which would eventually triumph over all man's efforts, with the structure of his body returning to the simple elements of the earth."3

After Adam and Eve sinned, God covered their nakedness with an animal skin, signifying the slaying and the shedding of blood of an innocent victim in place of the guilty. Their clothing would be a constant reminder of God's love and mercy and of His sparing their lives through the lifeblood of a *substitute.* This was the beginning of animal sacrifices as a way of restoring man to *inter-union* and *inter-communion* with Holy God and was a foreshadowing of a coming Redeemer Messiah, who would give His sinless blood for fallen humanity—the innocent dying for the guilty.

Chapter 5
THE BLOOD CRIES OUT

"For the life of the flesh is in the blood: and I have given it to you upon the altar to make atonement for your souls: for it is the blood that makes atonement for the soul." (Leviticus 17:11 NKJ)

Blood! It is the element in our bodies that gives physical life, but it is more than that. It is what makes you *you* through your DNA. Your DNA determines your genetic makeup: what you look like, your personality, the color of your hair, eyes, and even your intelligence. It can also be used to trace ancestry, convict criminals, and establish paternity. But what does our DNA have to do with our spiritual life and life after death? To understand this, we must focus on a most important aspect of life--blood covenanting. Every human being, whether they realize it or not, is in a blood covenant relationship with either God or Satan.

"In this the children of God are manifest, and the children of the devil: whosoever doeth not righteousness is not of God, neither he that loveth not his brother." (I John 3:10 KJV)

It is a known fact that the blood is the life and our heart, as the blood-fountain, is the very soul of our personality; therefore blood-transference is soul-transference and blood-sharing, whether human, or divine-human, brings about an inter-union of natures. That means a union of our human nature with God is the highest ultimate attainment we can reach as a human being. Even though blood covenanting has been practiced for centuries between two individuals or tribes (whether in the Middle East, Africa, Europe, or beyond), our Western culture as a whole has never grasped nor understood its meaning or importance. That being the case, and since it affects not only our life on earth but our destiny after death, I will try to shed some light on this rite, not only between humans but most importantly between God and man.

We know that *blood represents life*; therefore the *giving of blood* represents *the giving of life*. The *receiving of blood* represents *the receiving of life*. Today, the giving of blood through a blood transfusion is a common practice to save another's life, but this is not the same as entering into a blood covenant relationship with someone else that requires each participating party giving of their blood to the other. The *commingling of blood* between two parties represents *the commingling of natures*. The covenanting parties, after cutting their wrists or some other part of their bodies, would *commingle their bloods*, typifying the *commingling of their natures*. These acts sealed what is known as a *strong blood covenant friendship.*

People enter into blood covenant unions for different reasons: to make peace, for protection, to demonstrate deep caring for one another, and to protect against danger. Whatever the reason, the blood covenant is the most sacred, enduring, and binding rite on earth.

Before the covenant was cut (Hebrew: *berith, literally, to cut*) the parties would write down the agreements that were to be kept, cut themselves, commingle their bloods, take some of the blood and drink it, smear some on their agreements, place the agreements in amulets, and wear them around their necks or some other part of their bodies for the duration of their lives as a reminder of their *strong blood covenant friendship*.

Once the blood covenant was completed, the parties slew an animal, divided it in half, placed the halves opposite one other, and walked between the pieces, pledging themselves to "life and to death": life if they kept the covenant and death if they violated it. In other words, they were saying let what happened to the animal happen to me if I break the covenant. It was a "union in blood," to *life* or to *death*. Once all was completed, they had a covenant meal together. The *inter-union* in blood solidified the *inter-communion* of fellowship. The covenant was more binding than their relationships with their natural brothers and sisters.

In the Middle East, a blood covenanting partner is referred to as "a friend that sticks closer than a brother" (by birth). Westerners have heard the saying "blood is thicker than water," but the Middle East version is "blood is thicker than milk."1

Middle Easterners call two children nursed at the same breast "milk brothers," or "sucking brothers." The ties of such children are very strong. A boy and girl with this relationship cannot marry, even though by birth they may have no family relationship. But those who taste each other's blood are in a surer covenant than those who taste the same milk.2

BORNEO BLOOD BROTHERHOOD

"This covenant of blood-friendship is found in different parts of Borneo. In the days of Mr. Ellis, the Rev. W. Medhurst, a missionary of the London Missionary Society in Java, described it, in reporting a visit made to the Dayaks of Borneo, by one of his assistants, together with a missionary of the Rhenish Missionary Society.

Telling of the kindly greeting given to these visitors at a place called Golong, he says that the natives wished to establish a fraternal agreement with the missionaries, on condition that the latter should teach them the ways of God. The travelers replied, that if the Dayaks became the disciples of Christ, they would be constituted the brethren of Christ without any formal compact. The Dayaks, however, insisted that the travelers should enter into a compact (with them), according to the custom of the country, by means of blood. The missionaries were startled at this, thinking that the Dayaks meant to murder them, and committed themselves to their Heavenly Father, praying that whether living or dying, they might lie at the feet of their Savior. It appears, however, that is the custom of the Dayaks, when they enter into a covenant, to draw a little blood from the arms of the covenanting parties, and having mixed it with water, each to drink, in this way, the blood of the other.

Mr. Barenstein (one of the missionaries) having consented (for both) to the ceremony, they all took off their coats, and two officers came forward with small knives, to take a little blood out of the arm of each of them (the two missionaries and two Dayak chiefs). This being mixed together in four glasses of water, they drank, severally, each from the glass of the other;

after which they joined hands and kissed. The people then came forward, and made obeisance to the missionaries, as the friends of the Dayak King, crying out with loud voices, 'Let us be friends and brethren forever; and may God help the Dayaks to obtain the knowledge of God from the missionaries!' The two chiefs then said, 'Brethren, be not afraid to dwell with us, for we will do you no harm; and if others wish to hurt you, we will defend you with our life's blood, and die ourselves ere you be slain. God be witness, and this whole assembly be witness, that this is true.' Whereupon the whole company shouted. 'Balaak!' or 'Good, Be it so'."3

BLOOD COVENANTING

Blood covenanting dates back to the time of Adam in the Garden of Eden; although the word *covenant* is not found in the Bible until Genesis 6:18 concerning Noah, we must remember that Adam was in covenant oneness with God before he sinned and violated God's Word by partaking of the forbidden fruit. We must also remember that God used animal skins to clothe Adam's and Eve's nakedness, signifying that an animal, or animals, had to be slain because of their sin. This was the beginning of blood covenant sacrifices; the innocent animal was slain and its blood poured out as a substitute to bring fallen man back into inter-union and inter-communion with Holy God. The animal had to be slain to get to its *life*, which is *the blood*. In the Garden of Eden, God instituted the rite of blood covenanting between Adam, his seed, and Himself. This is verified in Genesis, chapter 4, pertaining to Cain and Abel.

THE RIGHT OFFERING

Cain and Abel were born unto Adam and Eve and were most certainly taught the ways of God. The Bible does not tell us how far from the Garden of Eden they lived, but its nearness would be a constant reminder of the cost their parents paid for their disobedience. God had determined, according to the Scriptures, a set time and place for Cain and Abel to offer sacrifices to maintain their blood covenant oneness with Him. Let us look at the account:

"And in the process of time it came to pass that Cain brought of the fruit of the ground an offering unto the LORD. And Abel, he also brought of the firstlings of his flock and of the fat thereof. And the LORD had respect unto Abel and to his offering: but unto Cain and to his offering he had not respect. And Cain was very wroth, and his countenance fell. And the LORD said unto Cain, Why art thou wroth? and why is thy countenance fallen? If thou doest well, shalt thou not be accepted? and if thou doest not well, sin lieth at the door. And unto thee shall be his desire, and thou shalt rule over him."
(Genesis 4:3-7 KJV)

These scriptures give us insight into three important reasons why God did not accept Cain's offering but accepted Abel's:

1. The offerings were supposed to be sacrificial offerings, which required the slaying of the animal, and its blood (*life*) offered up to God for inter-union, and inter-communion, not a bloodless gift of the fruit of the ground. Abel's offering of the *firstlings* of his flock and of the *fat* of the animal, was reflective of his love, devotion, and obedience to God, while Cain's offering revealed his deep-seated

rebellion against God. God gave him another chance to do right by bringing a blood sacrifice offering, but he did not.

2. Abel's offering of the *fat* of his sacrifice lets us know it was a blood covenant offering, as is verified in Leviticus 3:14-17 regarding God's instructions to Israel concerning sacrifices.

3. We also know the offerings were supposed to be sacrificial, according to Hebrews 11:4:

"By faith Abel offered to God a more excellent sacrifice than Cain, through which he obtained witness that he was righteous, God testifying of his gifts; and through it he being dead still speaks." (NKJ)

It was supposed to be a blood sacrifice which would allow Abel to be righteous in God's eyes. This is only accomplished through blood covenanting. Also, Abel offered his sacrifice *by faith*. How did he know to offer it *by faith*? The Bible says, *"faith cometh by hearing, and hearing by the Word of God."* (Hebrews 10:17 KJV) How did Abel hear the Word of God and know how to offer sacrifice? He learned from Adam; so did Cain, but Cain chose not to offer a proper, acceptable sacrifice. Abel and Cain, with their contrasting spirits and attitudes, would be the first participants to set in motion the prophecy of "The Two Twofold Seeds" of Genesis 3:15. *"And I will put enmity between you and the woman, and between your seed and her Seed; He shall bruise your head and you shall bruise His heel."* (NKJ)

The twofold seed of Satan:

1. Demons, evil spirits, fallen angels who bear Satan's nature (Matt. 25:41; Rev.12:3, 4, 7-9). (Wenham.)

2. Unredeemed men who bear Satan's nature (Matt. 13:38b; John 8:38-44; I John 3:8, 10, 12).

The twofold seed of the woman:
1. The Lord Jesus Christ (Gal. 3:16; Rev. 12:1-5, 13; Heb. 2:14; I John 3:8).
2. Redeemed men who bear God's nature (Rev. 12:5, 17; Matt. 13:38a; I John 3:1-2, 9-10a). (Calvin, Lange, Hamilton, etc.) 4

We know that the seed (sperm) comes from the man, not from the woman; but in this case the Seed is coming from Eve, which means there is going to be a supernatural, virgin birth of the coming Messiah.

Cain was in rebellion against God and in oneness with Satan. Filled with bitterness, hatred, and jealousy toward his brother because of Abel's holy walk and obedience to God, Cain devised a plan to commit premeditated murder:

"And Cain talked with Abel his brother: and it came to pass, when they were in the field, that Cain rose up against Abel his brother, and slew him." (Genesis 4:8 KJV)

The cosmic rebellion of Satan and his angels now becomes an earthly rebellion with the fall of Adam and Eve. Satan now begins to use his new confederate, Cain, to carry out his diabolical scheme of murder to try to abort God's promise of a coming Redeemer. The murder of Abel set off the war between the *"seed of the woman"* and the *"seed of the serpent."* The blood and DNA of Abel was spilled upon the earth; and it was not only Abel's blood, but the blood of his progeny.

"And the LORD said unto Cain, Where is Abel thy brother? And he said, I know not: Am I my brother's keeper? And he said, What hast thou done? the voice of thy brother's blood crieth unto me from the ground. And now art thou cursed from the earth, which hath opened her mouth to receive thy brother's blood from thy hand." (Genesis 4:9-11 KJV)

"Thy brother's blood" in Hebrew is *damey achikha*. It is plural and is translated as "thy brother's bloods." All the descendants that would have come from Abel's seed and bloodline were now cut off. Cain, in essence, committed multiple murders when he slew Abel.

Although Abel's blood was emptied from his body and poured out on the ground, it did not lose its vitality. The life that was in his blood was not destroyed, even though it was now separated from his body. God told Cain that the "voice of his brother's blood was crying up to Him from the ground." Even though Abel was dead physically, his blood was still living and had a voice. Why? Because *life* is *in the blood*.

LIVING BLOOD

Just like the story of Abel, other historical accounts document instances of murdered victims' blood crying out for revenge.

"There is a widespread belief that the blood of a murdered man will bear witness against the murderer by flowing afresh at his touch; the living blood crying out from the dead body, by divine consent, in testimony of crime against the Author of life.

Early in the sixteenth century during the rule of Christian of Denmark, who was called the 'Nero of the North,' several men had gathered in a tavern, and during the course of the evening, some of them began quarreling, a fight broke out, and someone was stabbed to death. Due to the number of people present, the murderer was unknown; but before the victim died he accused one of the king's attendants of being his assailant. The attendant denied the accusation; so in order to find out the truth, the king gathered all the men who had been present at the tavern, had them stand around the corpse, and one at a time, place their right hand on the dead man's chest and swear they had not killed him. One by one the men did so and no sign appeared against them. Finally, the only one left was the king's attendant. Because he was so condemned in his own conscience, he first of all kissed the dead man's feet. Then when he laid his hand upon the man's chest, immediately blood gushed forth in abundance, both out of his wound and nostrils. Urged by this evident accusation, the murderer confessed, and by the king's command was immediately beheaded."5

THE RIGHTEOUS VINDICATED
From the time of Abel until today, righteous men and women have died for their faith in God. Ungodly men have strewn their blood from one end of the earth to the other in mocking rebellion against God Almighty. One day soon the court of heaven will be opened and God will sit in judgment upon the ungodly. Every murderer from Cain to today's killer will stand before God to be tried. They will have no excuse because the blood of their victims will *cry out against them*.

The Hamans, Hitlers, and Stalins of the world will be there. Today the voices of the blood and DNA of every aborted child are crying out to God for justice (fifty-five million in the United States alone) and will stand as a testimony against our Supreme, Federal, and State Courts and their judges, as well as judges and courts of other nations which have approved abortion. Every doctor and nurse, and every man and woman who has taken part in snuffing out the lives of these unborn infants and have not asked God for forgiveness and made Jesus Christ Savior and Lord of their lives, will give an account of their actions before their Maker. Yes, there is a Judgment Day. There is a payday.

"For behold, the Lord is coming forth out of His place (heaven) to punish the inhabitants of the earth for their iniquity; the earth also will disclose the blood shed upon her, and will no longer cover her slain and conceal her guilt." (Isaiah 26:21 NKJ)

The blood and DNA of every righteous person who has given their life for their faith in Jesus Christ will be a witness against their slayers. Revelation 6:9-10 speaks of this:

"When He opened the fifth seal, I saw under the altar the souls of those who had been slain for the word of God and for the testimony which they held. And they cried with a loud voice, saying, How long, O Lord, holy and true, until You judge and avenge our blood on those who dwell on the earth?"

JERUSALEM CLEANSED
God is also going to purge the bloodstains from Jerusalem, Israel. For at least 3,500 years it has been a place of wars and

contention. It was the capital city of King David and the kings of Judah. It was the city where King Solomon built a temple unto God who dwelt in the Holy of Holies above the Mercy Seat. It was the place of our Savior, Jesus Christ's death, burial, and Resurrection. It was the city out of which went forth the gospel of salvation to the world by twelve Jewish Apostles. And it is the city to which our Savior, Jesus Christ, is going to return to set up His kingdom rule over the earth.

God chose Jerusalem for His habitation and gave it to the Jewish people as an everlasting possession through His blood covenants with Abraham, Moses, and Israel. Satan's purpose has been to try to destroy every semblance of God from the face of the earth. This includes Jerusalem, the state of Israel, and the Jewish people, as well as true followers of the Lord Jesus Christ. Many armies have marched against this holy city and razed it to the ground, but each time it has risen out of the dust as a testimony of God's covenant with Israel and His faithfulness as their Lord. God will one day soon cleanse His chosen city from all iniquity and bloodstains.

"And it shall come to pass that he who is left in Zion and he who remains in Jerusalem will be called holy, everyone who is recorded among the living in Jerusalem. When the Lord has washed away the filth of the daughters of Zion, and purged the blood of Jerusalem from her midst, by the spirit of judgment and by the spirit of burning." (Isaiah 4:3-4 NKJ)

ANGOLA PRISON
There are many instances where evil men and women who have committed murder and other heinous crimes have been

changed by giving their lives to Jesus Christ. A good example of this is in Angola Prison in Louisiana. Dr. Ravi Zacharias, the great Christian Apologist and head of Ravi Zacharias International Ministries, wrote in his *Newsletter Update* of his September 22, 2012, experience of being invited to speak at Angola Prison a week after speaking at the United Nations. I was so moved by his article and the hope it would give to others who might think there is no forgiveness for them because of their evil deeds, that I wanted to include it in my book. My wife and I have supported Dr. Zacharias' ministry for years, and I am so thankful for his work as he reaches out to the lost and intelligentsia of our generation, but most of all for his love for our Lord Jesus Christ. Here is Dr. Zacharias' firsthand account of his experience.

"Angola prison is on the Mississippi line, sixty miles north of the city of Baton Rouge, Louisiana. It comprises 18,000 acres and covers some twenty-two square miles. It is larger than Manhattan Island. The total prison population is about 5,300, 85% of whom are on life without parole. They will never see freedom again. Among these are about forty-five on death row. Escape is almost impossible; a large pack of dogs, some part wolf and part dog, with a heightened sense of smell are used to track a prisoner down should any dare try. Until a few short years ago, it was known as the bloodiest prison in the country. When a prisoner was brought in, he was given a knife to protect himself while within the prison. Imagine that! Blood stains were visible on the prison floors and walls. The place was brutal and survival in the world of criminals was itself a battle. It is a place that takes days to process in one's thinking. It is a place where crime has opened the door and hope shuts it. But then came a deeply committed Christian warden who wanted to change the place and Angola Prison

is now a place where 'Amazing Grace' can be and has been sung many times. How did this change come about? The new warden believed he had a call from God and his mission was to make a difference. Around this mission, he built his team. Now, instead of blood on the walls Scripture verses can be read on many walls and there are Bibles in many cells. Now one of the safest prisons in the country, no profanity is allowed by either staff or inmates. The power of the gospel to transform is so visible that even the secular state representatives recognize what has happened there. Listening to the prisoners leaves you deeply overwhelmed by how only God has changed these hearts. One of the men on our team remarked, 'If they would allow Bibles in our schools again, maybe we wouldn't need so many cells in our prisons.'

I spoke three times that day, to about one hundred inmates enrolled in a theological studies program, to the warden's key staff and chaplains, and finally, in the main auditorium, which was packed to capacity while the message was piped into every cell. At the invitation, many responded and gave their lives to Christ. It was the prisoners who led in the worship, providing the music and the singing...As I visited the execution room, I saw that even in the final moments of life, only the gospel can bring rescue to the forefront: In the room where the prisoner takes his last meal with the warden, the prisoners have painted two beautiful pieces; one is of Daniel kneeling in the lion's den, meaning, 'God can still rescue you'; the other is of Elijah riding on chariots of fire into the heavens, meaning, 'If you're not rescued here, you can meet him in heaven.' What hidden abilities God has imbedded even in those who have inherited and/or caused such extreme pain. Praying with some of them is an experience I will not forget. One mother called our office as I was literally on that twenty-mile road to the prison. Her son was serving a life sentence in Angola

Prison and she wondered if I could speak to him. Just before I spoke the warden brought him to me and sat him in the front row, and I had the privilege of seeing him come to Christ.

*As we flew back in that dark night, we were all profoundly moved and saw more clearly than ever how much our world is in need of the gospel message. Every day Angola continues to tug at my heart."*6

There is hope for the hopeless. If God can redeem these prisoners who have been condemned to life behind bars, He can redeem you.

WHAT ABOUT YOUR FUTURE?

What is your spiritual position in life right now? Are you under Satan's control, or have you committed your life to Jesus Christ? Are you serving Satan and his kingdom or God and His kingdom? There is no middle ground. "Disobedience to the Gospel is promoted by the devil, who holds unbelievers in spiritual darkness and death."7 Jesus' commission to the Apostle Paul was to go, not only to the Jews but also to the Gentiles, *"to open their eyes and turn them from darkness to light, and from the power of Satan to God, so that they may receive forgiveness of sins, and inheritance among them which are sanctified by faith that is in me."* (Acts 26:18)

Your blood is affected by your lifestyle and what you are devoted to. If you are part of God's kingdom and serving Him, it is reflected in your physical and spiritual being, plus it assures you of your future in heaven. People will know there is a difference in you. If you are part of Satan's kingdom, that will also be reflected in your physical and spiritual being. Your standards and lifestyle will reveal your allegiance to Satan. The Bible says the minds of unbelievers have been blinded by Satan to keep them from receiving God's Word that they might be saved.

"But even if our gospel is veiled, it is veiled to those who are perishing, whose minds the god of this age (Satan) has blinded, who do not believe, lest the light of the gospel of the glory of Christ, who is the image of God, should shine on them." (II Corinthians 4:3-4 NKJ. Emphasis mine.)

You do not have to continue living in darkness. You can even now be saved if you believe that Jesus Christ died for your sins, confess that you are a sinner and ask Him to come into your heart. He will not turn you away but will deliver you from the power of Satan and his kingdom, translating you into God's kingdom, giving you peace and making you a new person in Him. Colossians 1:12-14 says,

"Giving thanks to the Father who has qualified us to be partakers of the inheritance of the saints in the light. He has delivered us from the power of darkness and translated us into the kingdom of the Son of His love, in whom we have redemption through His blood, the forgiveness of sins." (NKJ)

Since God created you, He can wipe your slate clean in an instant and seal your eternal destiny in Him. Today you can change your life forever. The choice is yours.

Chapter 6
SOMEONE IS COMING

"I shall see him, but not now: I shall behold him but not nigh: There shall come a Star out of Jacob, and a Scepter shall rise out of Israel, and shall smite the corners of Moab, and destroy all the children of Sheth." (Numbers 24:17 KJV)

Cain's slaying of Abel did not negate God's promise of a coming Redeemer as Satan had hoped, for the Bible says that Eve bore another son and named him Seth, saying, *"God hath appointed me another seed instead of Abel, whom Cain slew."* (Genesis 4:25 KJV) Seth means *appointed* or *substituted*. God would use Seth to carry forward the godly line of the seed of the woman to further His plan in bringing forth the future Messiah Redeemer, Jesus Christ. It is interesting that Seth bore a son and called his name Enos; for it was then, according to Genesis 4:26, that *"men began to call upon the name of the LORD."* This is the first time the Bible speaks of public worship of God. During this time, Cain had departed from God's Presence, for God had pronounced judgment upon him for slaying his brother Abel.

"And now art thou cursed from the earth, which hath opened her mouth to receive thy brother's blood from thy hand. When thou tillest the ground, it shall not henceforth yield unto thee her strength; a fugitive and a vagabond shalt thou be in the earth. And Cain said unto the LORD, My punishment is greater than I can bear. Behold, thou hast driven me out this day from the face of the earth; and from

thy face shall I be hid; and I shall be a fugitive and a vagabond in the earth...". (Genesis 4:11-14 KJV)

Cain moved east of Eden to the land of Nod (which means *wandering),* bore a son named Enoch (not the Enoch from the godly lineage of Seth who was translated), built a city, and named it after his son. It was the beginning of urban development. Cain's objective was, along with his family, to take control of the earth and its possessions without God's help. This mindset, through Cain's descendants which were *the seeds of Satan,* would be passed on from generation to generation to our present day. Postmodernism, secular humanism, relativism, evolution, etc. were all born out of Cain's defiance of God. His life and actions were the seed bed of all that is anti-God, whereas Seth's descendants would carry forth the lineage of the godly seed.

THE GODLY SEED

As we trace the bloodline of Seth, we will address some of the three hundred prophecies of the coming Messiah which were written in the Scriptures by the Jewish prophets hundreds of years prior to Messiah's appearance. As I stated in a previous chapter, no other book or religion in the world has ever given a prophecy of its coming leader, written hundreds of years before he or she appeared on the scene. Nor have any ever prophesied beforehand regarding different aspects of his or her life that would be fulfilled exactly as had been spoken, or written of, by the Jewish prophets. Only the Bible can boast of that. The Bible prophecies began with Genesis 3:15 and continued with Seth and his progeny.

In chapter 5 of Genesis we find the genealogy of Seth, beginning with Adam. Seth's descendant, Enoch, was born of the seventh generation from Adam. Enoch means *dedicated*. The Bible tells us that Enoch "walked with God" and was God's prophet. He was a preacher of righteousness to his godless generation and was so holy that God *took him* (to heaven) after he lived 365 years. *"And Enoch walked with God: and he was not; for God took him."* (Genesis 5:24 KJV) A prime example of God's foreknowledge is that, although Enoch lived before the Flood, he prophesied (through the power of the Holy Spirit) of the Second Coming of the Messiah, Jesus Christ, which would happen thousands of years later. This is an astounding prophecy, as we will see later on.

"And Enoch also, the seventh from Adam, prophesied of these, saying, Behold the Lord cometh with ten thousands of his saints to execute judgment upon all, and to convince all that are ungodly among them of all their ungodly deeds which they have ungodly committed, and of all their hard speeches which ungodly sinners have spoken against him." (Jude 14-15 KJV)

This is the second in a line of prophecies of the coming Messiah which were spoken by a man who never died because he walked with God. Before his translation, Enoch bore a son and named him Methuselah. Methuselah then bore a son and named him Lamech, which means "to long for." Lamech bore a son and named him Noah, which means "to give comfort or grace." In the lives of Lamech and Noah and the meaning of their names, we see a longing desire for a coming Redeemer. Remember also that Methuselah was the son of Enoch.

Methuselah's name means "sent to die" or "when he dies it shall come." What does the "it shall come" mean?

The "it" means *the Flood*. Methuselah's name was a prophecy of the coming Flood upon the earth, which tells us that Enoch, Methuselah, Lamech, and Noah must have known of the coming Flood of judgment. Methuselah lived to be 969 years old; the year Methuselah died, the Flood came. Before God sent the Flood, He instructed Noah to build an ark in which to save his family plus the number of animals God would send both to repopulate the earth and provide for future sacrificial offerings.

A FLOOD TO SAVE

"The first age of human history was brought to its climax and culmination in the days of Noah. The sin-disease, which began so innocuously when Eve was tempted to doubt the word of God, which then began to show its true ugliness of character in the life of Cain, which came to maturity in the godless civilization developed by his descendants, finally descended into such a terrible morass of wickedness and corruption that only a global bath of water from the windows of heaven could purge and cleanse the fevered earth."[1]

"Then the Lord saw that the wickedness of man was great in the earth, and that every intent of the thoughts of his heart was only evil continually. And the Lord was sorry that He had made man on the earth, and He was grieved in His heart. So the Lord said, "I will destroy man whom I have created from the face of the earth, both man and beast, creeping thing and birds of the air, for I am sorry that I have made them." (Genesis 6:5-7 NKJ)

God was going to bring judgment upon the earth with a flood, but He would preserve Noah, a preacher of righteousness (II Peter 2:5), to carry forth the promise of a coming Redeemer Messiah. The Bible says in Genesis 6:8 (KJV) that *"Noah found grace in the sight of the Lord."* The entire human race would be destroyed in the Flood except Noah, his wife, his three sons, (Shem, Ham, and Japheth), and their wives. It is important to note that when Jesus Christ came the first time, His disciples asked Him *"what shall be the sign of thy coming, and of the end of the world?"* (Matthew 24:3 KJV) In verses 37-39, He says:

"But as the days of Noah were, so shall also the coming of the son of man (Jesus) be. For as in the days that were before the flood, they were eating and drinking, marrying and giving in marriage, until the day that Noah entered the ark and knew not until the flood came, and took them all away, so shall also the coming of the son of man be." (Emphasis mine.)

"Just as world conditions in the days before the Flood presaged a coming catastrophe, so will world conditions in the last days of this age foreshadow an even greater catastrophe. Some of these characteristics are summarized as follows:

(1) Preoccupation with physical appetites (Luke 17:27)
(2) Rapid advances in technology (Genesis 4:22)
(3) Grossly materialistic attitudes and interests (Luke 17:28)
(4) Uniformitarian philosophies (Hebrews 11:7)
(5) Inordinate devotion to pleasure and comfort (Genesis 4:21)
(6) No concern for God in either belief or conduct (II Peter 2:5; Jude 15)

(7) Disregard for the sacredness of the marriage relation (Matthew 24:38)
(8) Rejection of the inspired Word of God (I Peter 3:19)
(9) Population explosion (Genesis 6:1, 11)
(10) Widespread violence (Genesis 6:11, 13)
(11) Corruption throughout society (Genesis 6:12)
(12) Preoccupation with illicit sex activity (Genesis 4:19; 6:2)
(13) Widespread words and thoughts of blasphemy (Jude 15)
(14) Organized Satanic activity (Genesis 6:1-4)
(15) Promulgation of systems and movements of abnormal depravity (Genesis 6:5, 12).

These conditions prevailed in the days of Noah and they are all rapidly growing again today. There is good reason, therefore, to believe that these present times are those which immediately precede the return of the Lord Jesus Christ."2

It is amazing that the meanings of the names from Adam to Noah tell the prophetic story of a coming Redeemer Messiah.

English /Hebrew
Adam/Man
Seth/Substituted
Enos/Mortal
Cainan/Mourner
Mahalaleel/Blessed of God, Praise of God
Jared/Came Down
Enoch/Devoted
Methuselah/Sent to Die or, When He Dies It [the Flood] Comes
Lamech/Long For
Noah/To Give Comfort or Grace

When we put the meanings of their names together, we have a prophetic picture of the coming Messiah who would die for our sins and bring redemption to those who would love and obey Him:

MAN SUBSTITUTED A MORTAL MOURNER, A BLESSED (PRAISE OF GOD), CAME DOWN, DEVOTED (DEDICATED), SENT TO DIE, THE LONGING ONES TO COMFORT, (GIVE GRACE).3

Each of the above patriarchs carried forward the blood and DNA of the righteous lineage that would eventually bring forth the Jewish virgin who would be used of God to birth the Messiah.

Before the Flood, God instructed Noah to build an ark and bring his wife, three sons, their wives, and the animals into it to save them from the Flood. There were two reasons for this. One, the life (blood and DNA) which flowed through the animals would be used not only to repopulate the animal kingdom but also to become blood covenant sacrifices for covenantal relationships between God and man down through the centuries. Second, all the life (blood and DNA) which flowed through Noah and his family would be used not only to repopulate the earth but to ultimately bring forth the Messiah and redemption for all mankind. In other words, *in the ark was all the blood and DNA necessary to do all God had promised.* When the Flood came, that blood and DNA rose above the waters of destruction and the tides of evil and violence. After the waters subsided, God instructed Noah and his family to leave the ark.

The first thing Noah did was build an altar and offer a *blood sacrifice* for *inter-union* and *inter-communion* with holy God:

"Then Noah built an altar to the Lord of every clean animal and of every clean bird, and offered burnt offerings on the altar. And the Lord smelled a soothing aroma. Then the Lord said in His heart, "I will never again curse the ground for man's sake..." (Genesis 8:20-21 NKJ)

(For proof of Noah's Flood, Google "Scientific Proof of Noah's Flood." There are several sites that validate the Flood and debunk Evolution, strictly from a scientific and geological standpoint.)

THE TENTS OF SHEM
As we stated earlier, Noah had three sons—Shem, Ham and Japheth—that survived the Flood. Of these three, Shem, would be chosen as the righteous seed to carry on the bloodline and DNA that would later bring forth the Messiah Redeemer, Jesus Christ. Genesis 11:10-26 traces the lineage of Shem to Abram, and it would be through Abram (God later changed his name to Abraham, which means "Father of many nations") that the promises of God would begin to be fulfilled in detail.

Approximately 427 years after the Flood, around 2092 B.C., God called Abram out of Ur of Chaldee (what is now Iraq) and instructed him to go to the land of Canaan (the land of Israel); there God would bless him. Genesis 12:2-3, 7 says, *"And I will make of thee a great nation, and I will bless thee, and make thy name great; and thou shalt be a blessing: And I will bless them that bless thee, and curse him that curseth thee: and in thee shall all families of the earth be blessed. And the LORD appeared unto Abram, and said; unto thy seed will I give this land and there builded he an altar unto the LORD, who appeared unto him."*

God made five promises to Abram, based on the above verses:

1. God would bless him and make him a great nation. (Genesis 12:2)
2. God would make his name great and make him a blessing. (Genesis 12:2)
3. God would bless those who blessed him and curse those who cursed him. (Genesis 12:3)
4. God would bless all the families of the earth through Abram. (Genesis 12:3)
5. God would give the land of Canaan to Abram and his seed (Israel). (Genesis 12:7)

Genesis 14:13 tells us that Abraham was the first person to be called a Hebrew. It was an ethnic designation that came from his ancestor, Eber (Genesis 11:10-14), which means "to cross over."

Sometime later, God met with Abram and gave him instructions concerning a new blood covenant relationship. This covenant included more promises from God:

"And when Abram was ninety years old and nine, the LORD appeared to Abram, and said unto him, I am the Almighty God; walk before me, and be thou perfect. And I will make my covenant between me and thee and will multiply thee exceedingly. And Abram fell on his face: and God talked with him, saying, as for me, behold, my

covenant is with thee, and thou shalt be a father of many nations. Neither shall thy name any more be called Abram, but thy name shall be Abraham; for a father of many nations have I made thee. And I will make thee exceeding fruitful and I will make nations of thee and kings shall come out of thee. And I will establish my covenant between me and thee and thy seed after thee in their generations for an everlasting covenant, to be a God unto thee and to thy seed after thee. And I will give unto thee, and to thy seed after thee, the land wherein thou art a stranger, all the land of Canaan, for an everlasting possession; and I will be their God." (Genesis 17:1-8 KJV)

In the above verses, God tells Abraham that he would become the father of many nations. At the time, Abraham had no son, but God spoke to Abraham as if it were already done. This promise would be passed on through Abraham's first son, Isaac, then to Isaac's son, Jacob. From Jacob's bloodline and DNA would come the twelve tribes of Israel and their progeny. God also promised Abraham that kings would come out of his loins. This was another prophetic scripture regarding the future kings of Israel as well as the future King Messiah, Jesus Christ, who would one day rule the world.

This new covenant relationship between God and Abraham would be the covenant of circumcision, symbolizing Abraham and his seed's separation from the world and being covenanted unto God and His kingdom. It was the first time God had required the lineage of the righteous seed to shed blood for a covenant relationship:

"This is my covenant, which ye shall keep, between me and you and thy seed after thee; Every man child among you shall be circumcised.

And ye shall circumcise the flesh of your foreskin; and it shall be a token (sign) of the covenant betwixt me and you. And he that is eight days old shall be circumcised among you every man child in your generations..." (Genesis 17:9-14 KJV)

These descendants of Abraham would be known as the children of Israel, the Jewish people. God chose them for five basic reasons:

1. They were the chosen because of God's blood covenant with Abraham.
2. They were chosen to reveal God to the world and His plan for mankind.
3. They were chosen to preserve God's Holy Scriptures.
4. They were chosen to be a light of God's love and mercy to the nations.
5. They were chosen to bring forth the Jewish Messiah, Jesus Christ, the Savior of Israel and the world.

A KINGLY LINEAGE

As we progress through the prophetic Scriptures of the coming King Messiah, we come to Genesis 49:10. When Jacob was on his death bed, he called his twelve sons together and began to prophesy over each of them, telling them what would happen to them and their descendants in the future. Of the twelve tribes of Israel, Jacob singled out Judah (which means "praise") as the ruling tribe, the one through whom the Messiah King would come: *"The scepter shall not depart from Judah, nor a lawgiver from between his feet, until Shiloh comes, and to Him shall be the obedience of the people."* (NKJ) This Scripture would be fulfilled later when Jesus Christ the Messiah came. In his book

Evidence that Demands a Verdict, pages 176-77, Josh McDowell explains this most succinctly:

"Thus, according to this scripture and the Jews of their time, two signs were to take place soon after the advent of the Messiah:

1. removal of the scepter or identity of Judah
2. suppression of the judicial power (power to pass the death sentence).

The second chapter of Magath's book *Jesus before the Sanhedrin* is "The legal power of the Sanhedrin is restricted twenty-three years before the trial of Christ." All the nations which were subdued by the Roman Empire were deprived of their ability to pronounce capital sentences.

The *Talmud* itself admits that "a little more than forty years before the destruction of the Temple, the power of pronouncing capital sentences was taken away from the Jews." (*Talmud*, Jerusalem, Sanhedrin, fol. 24. recto.) Rabbi Rachmon says, "When the members of the Sanhedrin found themselves deprived of their right over life and death, a general consternation took possession of them; they covered their heads with ashes, and their bodies with sackcloth, exclaiming: 'Woe unto us for the scepter has departed from Judah, and the Messiah has not come!'"4

The Jewish Messiah, Jesus Christ, had come, walked among them, and taught them the Scriptures He had given to prophets down through the centuries concerning Himself; yet they did not recognize Him.

Centuries after Jacob's death and the prophecy he had given to Judah, the Jewish people found themselves in bondage to Pharaoh in Egypt. They dwelt there for 400 years; then God sent Moses, of the tribe of Levi, to deliver them and bring them into the land of Canaan as He had promised Abraham. God entered into a blood covenant relationship with Israel as a nation at Mt. Sinai, called the Mosaic Covenant, and then took them into Canaan to possess the land. God chose Jerusalem, then called Salem, as His blood covenant capitol city for the nation of Israel:

For the Lord has chosen Zion; He has desired it for His habitation: "This is My resting place forever; here I will dwell, for I have desired it." (Psalm 132:13-14 NKJ)

It was in Jerusalem that God began to institute His plans for an eternal kingship under Messiah by raising up King David from the tribe of Judah. The people of Israel had chosen their first king, Saul, of the tribe of Benjamin, based on their fleshly desires. When Saul rebelled against God, He removed him from his kingship and put in place His choice as king of Israel— King David, of the tribe of Judah, a man after God's own heart. The tribe of Judah was the bloodline God had originally chosen to bring forth the Jewish Messiah.

It was during King David's reign that God gave him another prophetic scripture concerning the future kingship of Israel. God told him his "house, throne, and kingdom" would be established forever (II Samuel 7:12-13.). This prophecy was a reference to Messiah, who would come through David's lineage. The Jewish prophet Jeremiah, who lived during the last of the kings of Judah, wrote of the coming King Messiah:

"Behold, the days are coming," says the Lord, "That I will raise to David a Branch of righteousness; a King shall reign and prosper, and execute judgment and righteousness in the earth. In His days Judah will be saved, and Israel will dwell safely; now this is His name by which He will be called: THE LORD OUR RIGHTEOUSNESS." (Jeremiah 23:5-6 NKJ)

This Messiah, Jesus Christ, would come to earth the first time not to establish an earthly kingdom but a spiritual one. He would be born and live in Israel, work mighty miracles, suffer death by crucifixion, be raised from the dead and conquer death, hell and the grave; thus He would forever seal God's promises from Adam to King David, to the nation of Israel, and to the Gentiles. He would one day return to Jerusalem, Israel, and establish His kingdom rule over the nations of the world.

Upon King David's death, his son Solomon became king in Israel. Solomon's name means "peaceful," but the Jewish prophet Nathan called him *Jedidiah*, which means "beloved of Jehovah." His names are indicative of Solomon and his forty-year reign in Israel. Both of his names and their meanings are reflective of the coming Jewish Messiah King who would be the "Prince of Peace" and "Beloved of Jehovah." This brings us to one of the most important prophetic scriptures in the Bible concerning Messiah, for it depicts Him as being born as a baby yet being God.

"For unto us a child is born, unto us a Son is given: And the government shall be upon his shoulder: And his name shall be called Wonderful, Counselor, The mighty God, The everlasting Father, The Prince of Peace. Of the increase of his government and peace there shall be no end, upon the throne of David and upon his kingdom, to order it, and to stablish it with judgment and with justice from henceforth even for ever. The zeal of the LORD of host will perform this." (Isaiah 9:6-7 KJV)

What is most interesting and of greatest importance is that the kings of Judah were representatives of God on earth, sitting upon His throne that would eventually become Messiah's in the future. Before King David died, he made his son Solomon king in his stead. I Chronicles 29:23, KJV, relates this:

*"Then Solomon sat on **the throne of the Lord** as king instead of David his father, and prospered; and all Israel obeyed him."*(Emphasis mine.)

When the Queen of Sheba came to visit King Solomon, she was astounded at his wealth, his wisdom, his ministers, and his servants, to the point that there was no more spirit left in her. In other words, it took her breath away to see who he was and what he had. She also, somehow, understood that Solomon was sitting on God's throne, ruling over Israel.

*"And when the Queen of Sheba had seen the wisdom of Solomon, and the house that he had built, and the meat of his table, and the sitting of his servants, and the attendance of his ministers, and their apparel; his cupbearers also, and their apparel; and his ascent by which he went up into the house of the LORD; there was **no more spirit in***

*her. And she said to the king, It was a true report that I heard in mine own land of thine acts, and of thy wisdom...**Blessed be the LORD thy God, which delighted in thee to set thee on his throne, to be king for the LORD thy God:** because thy God loved Israel, to establish them for ever, therefore made he thee king over them, to do judgment and justice."* (II Chronicles 9:3-5, 8 KJV. Emphasis mine.)

The kings of Israel were supposed to execute righteousness and justice for the nation of Israel, but later many of them became evil, turning away from God to serve idols, as did most of Israel. That is why God dealt so harshly with them and caused the northern tribes to be carried away as captives to Assyria, and later, the tribe of Judah to be taken captive to Babylon.

Years later, they would be back in the land of Israel under Persian, Greek, and finally under Roman rule. It was during Roman domination that Herod the Great was made king in Israel. He was not Jewish but an Edomite, and it was during his rule that God's promise to Adam and Eve, that the Seed of the woman would bruise the head of the Serpent (Satan), would be fulfilled. The bloodline and DNA of the godly seed had been preserved down through the centuries, although Satan had tried time and again to destroy it. Would he try again? Yes, several times but he would not succeed.

Chapter 7
THE DNA AND VIRGIN BIRTH

"Therefore the Lord Himself will give you a sign: behold, the virgin shall conceive and bear a Son, and shall call His name Immanuel."
(Isaiah 7:14 NKJ)

Several millennia had passed since God had given the promise of a coming Redeemer to Adam and Eve. Now the time had come for that promise to be fulfilled. Now the battle of the ages would begin between the Seed of the woman and Satan. God was going to perform a miracle in the birth of the Jewish Messiah by using the womb of a Jewish virgin girl by the name of Mary. Mary lived in the small town of Nazareth in northern Israel, west of the Sea of Galilee, and was from the lineage of King David through his son Nathan. She was engaged to a Jewish man named Joseph who also lived in Nazareth. Joseph, too, was from the lineage of King David but through David's son Solomon. Both Mary and Joseph were descendants of royalty. The Bible doesn't tell us how they happened to be living in Nazareth or how Joseph, being from kingly lineage, wound up being a carpenter. Regardless, God was going to use Mary to perform one of His greatest miracles ever. We find the narrative in the gospel of Luke:

"And in the sixth month the angel Gabriel was sent from God unto a city of Galilee, named Nazareth, to a virgin espoused to a man whose name was Joseph, of the house of David; and the virgins name was Mary...And the angel said unto her, Fear not Mary: for thou hast

found favour with God. And behold thou shalt conceive in thy womb, and bring forth a son and shalt call his name JESUS. He shall be great, and shall be called the Son of the Highest: and the Lord God shall give unto him the throne of his father David: And he shall reign over the house of Jacob forever; and of his kingdom there shall be no end. Then said Mary unto the angel, How shall this be, seeing I know not a man? And the angel answered and said unto her, The Holy Ghost shall come upon thee, and the power of the Highest shall overshadow thee: therefore also that holy thing which shall be born of thee shall be called the Son of God...For with God nothing shall be impossible. And Mary said, Behold the handmaid of the Lord; be it unto me according to thy word. And the angel departed from her."
(Luke 1:26-27, 30-35, 37-38 KJV)

A virgin birth was essential in order to redeem sinful man. As I stated in chapter three, because of disobedience to God's Word and eating of the forbidden fruit, the sin nature entered Adam and Eve's blood system. Therefore, every child that would be born on this earth would come from the seed of Adam, except Jesus Christ and thus would inherit the same sin nature as Adam. All of humanity is related by blood to Adam and Eve. The Scriptures are very clear on this:

*"And hath made of **one blood** all nations of men for to dwell on all the face of the earth..."* (Acts 17:26 KJV)

"For since by man came death, by man came also the resurrection of the dead. For as in Adam all die, even so in Christ shall all be made alive." (I Corinthians 15:21-22 KJV)

"Therefore as by the offense of one (Adam) judgment came upon all men to condemnation;...For as by one man's disobedience many were made sinners..." (Romans 5:18-19 KJV) (Emphasis mine.)

"For all have sinned and come short of the glory of God." (Romans 3:23 KJV)

"For the wages of sin is death; but the gift of God is eternal life through Jesus Christ our Lord." (Romans 6:23 KJV)

DNA

It would take pure, sinless blood to redeem mankind, which brings us to the core of this book. How could Jesus be born of Mary, even though she was a virgin, without her blood and DNA being passed on to Him? We will explain this mystery using medical science, beginning with conception and childbirth and concluding with Jesus' supernatural conception and childbirth. In Chapter 1, I touched on the meaning of DNA, but I want to elaborate on it here regarding conception.

According to *Webster's Dictionary*, DNA (deoxyribonucleic acid) is "an essential component of all living matter and a basic material in the chromosomes of the cell nucleus: it contains the genetic code and transmits the hereditary pattern."

In other words, DNA is the name of a long molecule in the center of a living cell that contains all the information that makes you who you are, determines what you look like, and more. Our genes create the chromosomes, of which there are 46 sets in the human body, arranged in 23 pairs. At conception, one set of chromosomes comes from the father and one set from the mother. Females have two X chromosomes in their cells, and males have one X and one Y. If the male sperm carrying an X chromosome reaches the female egg first, which carries only the X chromosome, the XX chromosomes produce a girl. If the male Y chromosome reaches the egg first, then the XY chromosomes produce a boy.

Human development begins when a male gamete (sperm) penetrates a female gamete (ovum) which then becomes a zygote (a cell formed by the union of male and female gametes). This is very interesting because *gamete*, in the Greek, means "wife"; *gametes* means "husband"; and *gamein* means "to marry." In the case of DNA, it is "a reproductive cell that is haploid (having the full number of chromosomes normally occurring in the mature germ cell) and can unite with another gamete to form the cell (zygote) that develops into a new individual" (*Webster's Dictionary*). In other words, the two gametes, male and female cells, marry. That is why two men or two women cannot have children. It was not God's design. He established the principle of reproduction in men's and women's blood systems, and every baby that has been or ever will be born—with the exception of Jesus Christ—has had his or her blood system and genetics passed down from generation to generation from an original human source, Adam and Eve.

TYPES OF CONCEPTION
There are those who do not believe in the virgin birth of Jesus Christ saying it is a myth, but I want to use some examples of conception that take place every day that do not require sexual intercourse between a man and woman. These methods will give us a better understanding of how the Lord Jesus could be

born of a virgin, without Mary having sexual relations with a man, in order for Him not to inherit man's sin nature. These human methods still take a male sperm and female egg, but they will at least help enlighten our minds regarding Jesus' supernatural conception.

1. In Vitro Fertilization: In Vitro Fertilization is the process in which a woman's (or a female donor's) egg is joined with the male sperm (either her husband's or another male's) and through a

2. the fertilization process becomes an embryo. It is then transferred to the woman's uterus; eight weeks later, if successful, the embryo becomes a fetus (baby) which continues to grow in the mother's womb until the time of delivery.

2. Artificial insemination: Artificial insemination is the process in which active, motile sperm are put directly into the uterus or cervix. There are a few preliminary steps that have to be taken before the injection to ensure a greater promise of success in producing a baby.

3. GIFT: GIFT is the acronym for Gamete Intrafallopian Transfer. Eggs are taken from the woman (or female donor) along with sperm from the man (or male donor) and placed in the fallopian tube; if successful, this procedure will produce a fetus which becomes a baby.

4. ZIFT: ZIFT is the acronym for Zygote Intrafallopian Transfer. As in GIFT, eggs and sperm are retrieved from the female and male. They are then fertilized in the lab via In

Vitro Fertilization and become zygotes. They are then placed in the woman's fallopian tube and, if successful, become a fetus which will produce a baby.

Notice that these procedures do not require the mother's eggs or the father's sperm but can use the eggs and sperm of donors. This is a very important point to remember in dealing with the virgin birth of Jesus Christ, because if donors are used, no sexual encounter between the man and woman is needed to produce the baby. The other important thing to remember is that the eggs and sperm come from human beings, which means that the baby will be born with Adam's sin nature, passed on through the blood and DNA. All of the above procedures take place without sexual intercourse between a man and woman.

In the case of the birth of our Lord Jesus Christ, there was no human male gamete (sperm) that penetrated the gamete (ovum) of the Jewish virgin Mary, and fertilized the egg which passed from the fallopian tube into the uterus and attached itself to become a fetus (baby). It was the *Holy Spirit* that overshadowed Mary and *implanted the holy seed of Jesus* in her *womb* supernaturally:

"And behold, thou shalt conceive in thy womb, and bring forth a son, and shalt call his name JESUS." (Luke 1:31 KJV.)

This in itself is miraculous, since normal conception takes place in the fallopian tube, not in the womb. This is confirmed again in Luke 2:21:

"And when eight days were accomplished for the circumcising of the child, his name was called JESUS, which was so named of the angel before he was conceived in the womb." (KJV)

We must remember that none of today's fertilization procedures were known at the time of Mary's conception of Jesus. As I stated before, the process of *In Vitro Fertilization* implants the embryo in the uterus, and, if successful, after 7 or 8 days becomes a fetus (baby). Before the baby was formed, the cells divided into two parts, forming the placenta (a type of container for the baby) and the baby. The placenta then attaches itself to the mother's uterine wall. The umbilical cord (which forms from the baby) attaches to the placenta and connects the baby to the mother. The umbilical cord is made up of two arteries and a large vein. The arteries pump blood from the baby's heart into the placenta vessels, which then send it to the uterine vessels. This process, known as osmosis, takes away the waste products from the baby, while the vein supplies the blood which is full of nutrients and oxygen to it. The blood which flows in an unborn baby's arteries and veins is not derived from the mother; it is produced within the body of the baby. No blood appears until after the baby has begun to develop. Medical science has shown that none of the mother's blood is given to a developing baby. She supplies the baby's nutrients, but no blood ever passes from the mother to the baby unless some abnormality develops, which in most cases causes a miscarriage. The baby generates its own blood, made up of plasma, red cells, white cells, and platelets. These are all produced by the bone marrow, liver and spleen, while the blood type comes from both the father and mother through the genes.

Now let us get back to the Virgin Birth of Jesus Christ. Mary supplied the womb and nourished His body, but her sin-tainted blood—since she was from the seed of Adam—was not passed on to Him. It was the Holy Spirit, not a man, who supplied the seed for Jesus' conception. God provided a way for Jesus to have a human body, but His genes were not from a human father and mother; they were supernaturally generated by God. His blood was produced within Himself, by His bone marrow, liver, and spleen, as pure, sinless blood; and the placenta and fetus were formed when the cells divided. His umbilical cord was produced from His own little body: therefore, He was a separate entity from Mary in her womb in every way, except being attached to her uterine wall in order to draw nourishment from her and excrete waste products.

We must remember that if God created the earth and the universe and created Adam out of the dust of the earth and Eve out of one of Adam's ribs and placed within their reproductive organs the ability to produce sperm and eggs, and if our medical profession can produce babies through the procedures mentioned above, then it was certainly possible for God to produce the embryo of Jesus, place it in the womb of Mary to become a baby, and have her body nourish Him until He was born. Again, it was all God. Mary was just the vessel God used to bring forth the Jewish Messiah Redeemer. It was a supernatural act of the Holy Spirit.

Doctors cannot create a sperm and egg from nothing; only God can do that. Let us recap all of this regarding conception without sexual relations between a man and woman:

1. Fertilization between the male sperm and female egg can take place in a laboratory.
2. The embryo is placed in the uterus by a doctor to be attached to the uterine wall.
3. The cells divide, producing a placenta and fetus (baby). The baby produces the umbilical cord.
4. The placenta attaches itself to the uterine wall and the umbilical cord to the placenta.
5. The umbilical cord is used to receive nourishment and oxygen from the mother and to take away waste products from the baby. No blood is exchanged between the mother and baby.
6. The baby produces its own blood from the marrow, liver, and spleen; the belief that babies' blood comes from the father is not true.
7. The genes, half from the father and half from the mother, make up the baby's DNA.
8. Because the baby is born from two humans who inherited their sin nature from Adam and Eve, the baby will have the same sin nature.

Now let us compare the conception of Jesus with the above details.

1. God prepared the embryo (Jesus) supernaturally, outside of Mary's womb.
2. The Holy Spirit overshadowed the virgin Mary and implanted the embryo (Jesus) in her womb.
3. The cells divided, becoming a fetus (baby Jesus) and placenta. The baby Jesus produced an umbilical cord.
4. Jesus' placenta attached itself to Mary's uterine wall and His umbilical cord to His placenta.

5. Jesus' umbilical cord received nourishment and oxygen from Mary and took away the waste products, but no blood was exchanged between Mary and Jesus.
6. Jesus produced His own blood from His marrow, liver, and spleen. His blood did not come from an earthly father or mother.
7. His genes came from God, not from man.
8. Because He was not conceived by two humans but by the Holy Spirit, He did not inherit the sin nature of Adam and Eve. He would be sinless, and His pure, sinless blood would be used to redeem fallen man, as well as all of creation.

LIFE IN THE WOMB

There is much controversy today concerning when a baby's life begins. Is it at conception, when it becomes an embryo, after it is fetus, or at birth? The pro-abortion movement, which is primarily a tool used by Satan to destroy human lives, does not believe that a baby is a human being until it is born. But is that true? What do medicine, God, and the Bible have to say about it?

Medical research has shown that a fetus can recognize its mother's voice. A study was conducted by Barbara Kisilevsky, a nursing professor of Queens University in Ontario, Canada, along with Chinese and Canadian researchers, that was published in the *Journal of Psychological Science* in 2003 (Although I am not quoting the article, I give it credit for the following information). They tested sixty pregnant women and tape recorded them reading a poem out loud. They separated the women into two groups of thirty and played the poem to each group. When a baby heard its mother's voice, its heart rate increased, but when they played the tape of another pregnant woman's voice, its heart rate slowed down. The baby did not recognize the voice of another woman and was trying to figure out who it was. The researchers also concluded that while the baby was still in the womb, its brain was learning patterns of speech and preparing for language acquisition after birth. All of this proves, medically, that the fetus is a real person.

The Bible tells us in the book of Jeremiah, Chapter 1 verses 4-5, that God chose and ordained Jeremiah to be a prophet to the nations before he was even born.

"Then the word of the LORD came unto me saying, Before I formed thee in the belly I knew thee; and before thou camest forth out of the womb I sanctified thee, and I ordained thee a prophet unto the nations."

There is an even more astounding story regarding embryos and fetuses being real persons in the gospel of Luke 1:39-45. The Jewish virgin, Mary, had just been visited by the angel Gabriel and was told she would become pregnant, supernaturally, by the power of the Holy Spirit, and would birth Jesus, the Jewish Messiah. After this event, Mary went to the home of her cousin Elizabeth to tell her the news.

"And Mary arose in those days, and went into the hill country with haste, into a city of Judah; and entered into the house of Zacharias, and saluted Elisabeth. And it came to pass that, when Elisabeth heard the salutation of Mary, the babe leaped in her womb; and Elisabeth was filled with the Holy Ghost: And she spake out with a loud voice,

and said, "Blessed art thou among women, and blessed is the fruit of thy womb. And whence is this to me, that the mother of my Lord should come to me? For lo as soon as the voice of thy salutation sounded in mine ears, the babe leaped in my womb for joy..."

In these scriptures, three important things are taking place. First, both women are pregnant. Elisabeth carried John, who was a fetus (baby) and would later be called John the Baptist and become the forerunner of Jesus Christ; and Mary carried Jesus Christ, an embryo (baby) which would become the Savior of the world.

Second, when Mary entered Elisabeth's home and greeted her, John—from inside Elisabeth's womb—*leaped for joy*. How astounding is that? Here are two babies somehow communicating with one another while in their mother's wombs. John was *leaping for joy* in the presence of his Creator and Messiah. In later years, after John and Jesus began their ministries, John, knowing his time of ministry and life on earth was drawing to a close as the forerunner of Jesus the Messiah, declared to his disciples, "...*my joy therefore is fulfilled. He (Jesus) must increase, but I must decrease.*" (John 3:29-30 KJV. Emphasis mine.)

Third, Elisabeth, being filled with the Holy Spirit, knew, by the Word of Knowledge (one of the gifts of the Holy Spirit), that Mary was carrying God the Son in her womb before Mary could break the news to Elisabeth about her miraculous conception. It was all a supernatural encounter and proof that babies in their mother's wombs are living, breathing, intelligent beings with a future and purpose for being born.

A BODY FOR MESSIAH

Jesus Christ took on a human body that God prepared for Him, yet He was still Divine, even in His humanity. His body was the vessel used by God to carry the precious, sinless, life-giving blood that would redeem fallen man.

*"Wherefore when he cometh into the world, he saith, ...**a body thou hast prepared me.**"* (Hebrews 10:5 KJV. Emphasis mine.)

John 1:14 sheds more light on this:

*"And the Word was made flesh and dwelt among us (and we beheld his glory, the glory as of **the only begotten of the Father.**) full of grace and truth."* (KJV. Emphasis mine.)

There are two things in this verse that catch our attention. One, "He was made flesh." The phrase "was made flesh" indicates a transition. In other words, He existed before He came to earth as a human. Two, according to *Vines Expository Dictionary of New Testament Words*, the phrase "the only begotten of the Father" means "that as the Son of God He was the sole representation of the Being and character of the One who sent Him...We can only understand the term 'the only begotten' when used of the Son, in the sense of unoriginated relationship. 'The begetting is not an event of time, however remote, but a fact irrespective of time. The Christ did not become, but necessarily and eternally is the Son.'"[1]

Jesus Christ came to earth, was born of a virgin, and took on a human body; but He was still different. How? The Bible tells us:

"Forasmuch then as the children are partakers of flesh and blood, he also himself likewise took part of the same; that through death he might destroy him that had the power of death, that is the devil; and deliver them who through fear of death were all their lifetime subject to bondage." (Hebrews 2:14-15 KJV)

The Greek word for "partakers" is *koinoneho*, which means "to fully partake." It means that all of Adam's descendants are of both his flesh and blood. The words "took part," as applying to Jesus Christ, is the Greek word "metecho" which means "to take part but not all." Jesus took on the flesh part of Adam but not his blood and sin nature. Only He is our Savior Redeemer.

PART II: THE VIRGIN BIRTH
Is Jesus Christ God's Son?

In concluding this chapter on the virgin birth, I want to address the issue of Jesus being the Son of God, especially since the Jewish rabbis and Muslims do not believe it. They say it is blasphemy, for God would have had to have a consort to have a Son. But is that true? Let's look at the Scriptures and Suras of the Koran.

In the genealogies of both the Old and New Testaments, we find the word "begat" used in describing the offspring of the person named before. For example, in Genesis 5:3, 6, it says, "Adam...begat Seth; Seth begat Enos," and so on, through the entire chapter. In Matthew Chapter 1 we see the same thing. "Abraham begat Isaac; Isaac begat Jacob; and Jacob begat Judah." This continues through verse 16, then something changes. Notice what it says: *"And Jacob* [not Isaac's Jacob] *begat Joseph the husband of Mary, of whom was born Jesus, who is called Christ."* (KJV) (Emphasis mine.) Did you notice that Joseph did not "beget" Jesus Christ, but He was "born" of Mary? Let me explain.

The similarity of the words "begot" or "begotten" in the Semitic languages will give us the key in unlocking this mystery regarding Jesus Christ being the Son of God.

"Begot" or "Begotten" in the Semitic and Greek languages: Arabic is youlad, Aramaic is yalad, or awled & ettled, Hebrew is yalad and Greek is gennao.

Each of these words, used in the Bible and the Koran for *begot* or *begotten*, are masculine causative verbs, except the Aramaic word *ettled*, which is feminine passive. All the words but *ettled*

denote's the male sexual organ. The Greeks translated both Aramaic words *awled* and *ettled* interchangeably as one Greek work, *gennao*. The problem arises when describing the birth of Jesus Christ using *gennao*; the birth of Jesus (*Isa* in the Koran) would then be seen as causative i.e., conceived biologically. Worse yet, using this term in the masculine sense depicts Jesus' birth as occurring through a divine male sexual act

The only exception to this universal use of *begot* is in the original Aramaic version when referring to the conception of Jesus Christ. The Gospel establishes the genealogy of Jesus by an extensive listing of who was begotten by whom, from Abraham, all the way to Joseph, the husband of Mary (Matthew 1:1-16). However, the Aramaic word changes from *awled* (male descendent, conceived through a male) to *ettled* (female descendent, supernaturally conceived through a female), when the lineage describes the birth of Jesus. This word literally means *he who is from her*, or in context, *Jesus that is from Mary*. This draws a profound distinction between the *awled*, begotten physically by a man, with *ettled*, begotten supernaturally by a woman. Ettled is a feminine passive term

96

suggesting that a man is not required for the conception process, implying a supernatural birth, or *begot*.2

Jesus' conception in Mary's womb was not through a human father, but by the Holy Spirit of God Himself. It was supernatural. The Holy Spirit (*Ruach Kodesh* in Hebrew, Rohch *Allah* in Qur'anic Arabic) of God brought this about. Matthew 1:18 tells us that Mary "...*was found with child of the Holy Ghost.*" The Koran also says that the conception of Jesus Christ would be supernaturally brought about by the *Rohch Allah* (Holy Spirit) (see Suras 3:47; 3:59; 5:110; 19:20; and 21:91). Therefore, the Bible and the Koran both agree on this. Psalm 2:7-8 tells us that God has a Son:

"I will declare the decree: The Lord hath said unto me, Thou art my Son; this day have I begotten thee. Ask of me, and I shall give thee the heathen for thine inheritance, and the uttermost parts of the earth for thy possession." (KJV)

"Son...begotten thee, in the ancient Near East was a relationship between a great king and one of his subject kings, who ruled by his authority and owed him allegiance and was expressed not only by the words *lord* and *servant* but also by *father* and *son*. The Davidic king was the Lord's 'servant' and His 'son' (2 Samuel 7:5, 14). The word 'begotten' indicates the initiation of this relationship on the day of the King's coronation. This passage does not teach that Jesus the Son is 'begotten' (created/born) of the Father or that the Father eternally generates the Son."3 God is declaring that Jesus, being God the Son and the Creator of everything (John 1:1-3) has the right of inheritance over all of His creation.

THE DNA OF JESUS CHRIST

Then, in Psalm 110:1, the Jewish King David speaks of the coming Messiah as being God also.

"The LORD said unto my Lord, Sit thou at my right hand, until I make thine enemies thy footstool." (KJV)

Jesus used this verse in Matthew 22:41-46 regarding Himself as God's Son:

While the Pharisees were gathered together Jesus asked them, saying, "What do you think about the Christ? Whose Son is He?" They said to Him, "The Son of David." He said to them, "How then does David in the Spirit call Him 'Lord,' saying: 'The LORD said to my Lord, Sit at My right hand, till I make Your enemies Your footstool?' (NKJ)

"After answering three questions posed by Israel's religious leaders (vv. 15-22; 23-33; 34-40), Jesus turned to the Pharisees with a question of His own. The question had two parts, a first about the identity of the Messiah and a second about the interpretation of Psalm 110.

The answer to Jesus' question about the identity of the Messiah was in a number of OT passages (see 2 Sam. 7:12-16; Ps. 89:3, 4, 34-36; Is. 9:7; 16:5; 55:3, 4). The Messiah would come from David's royal line.

Verse 43 affirms that David wrote Psalm 110. Furthermore, it declares that David wrote the psalm under the inspiration of the Spirit. It also quotes Psalm 110:1, describing Christ's presence in heaven until He comes to reign on earth (see Hebrews 10:11-13; Rev. 3:21).

Psalm 110 seems to be completely prophetic and messianic, and uses two different words for God. The first, translated LORD, is the name Yahweh, the proper name of Israel's God. The second Lord means 'Master.' David, the great King of Israel, calls one of his offspring 'Lord' or 'Master,' a title for deity. The implication is that Jesus, the Son of David, is God. He is a descendant of David and therefore human, but He is also divine."4

God the Son came to earth and walked and lived among men. He ate with, slept with, drank with, and brought salvation to His own creation. He was the manifest glory of God on earth, healing the sick, casting out devils, walking on water, raising the dead, and exhibiting the power He used to create the universe and all that is in it. He was full of grace and truth. Although He was sinless, He had to die and be raised from the dead for you and me to have eternal life, and He is coming back soon!

Chapter 8
BORN TO DIE

"But when the fullness of time had come, God sent forth His Son, born of a woman, born under the law, to redeem those who were under the law, that we might receive the adoption as sons." (Galatians 4:4, KJV)

History, as well as the Bible, tells us that Jesus Christ was born in Bethlehem, Israel, sometime between 5 and 7 B.C. King Herod the Great, who was an Edomite, was off to war in 5 B.C. and died in 4 B.C. He had all male babies, aged two years and under, killed before he went to war to try to destroy Jesus, which gives us the timeline of His birth.

It was a tumultuous time for the Jewish people. Rome was in control of the land of Israel, taxes were extremely high, and the religious leadership was, for the most part, corrupt. Yet it was during this time of great difficulty that the expectation of a coming Messiah was running very high. Scriptures had been fulfilled predicting the time of His coming and now everything was set for His birth to take place. A census had been mandated by the Roman government, requiring that everyone should return to their place of birth to be registered, which for Joseph and Mary was Bethlehem, Israel. It was there, in Bethlehem (which means "The house of Bread"), that the Son of God, Jesus Christ, was born of Mary, a virgin. The place of His birth is very significant, in that He would be the "Bread of

Life" that would feed a dying world the Word of Truth and bring forth salvation to those who would believe in Him.

The events that unfolded on the day of Jesus' birth were of great significance. The Bible tells us that after Jesus was born, Mary wrapped Him in swaddling clothes.

"And she brought forth her firstborn son, and wrapped him in swaddling clothes and laid him in a manger..." (Luke 2:7 KJV)

Swaddling clothes were burial clothes which would be a "sign" to the shepherds, as announced by the angel when he appeared to them:

"And there were in the same country shepherds abiding in the field, keeping watch over their flock by night And lo, the angel of the Lord came upon them, and the glory of the Lord shone round about them: and they were sore afraid. And the angel said unto them, Fear not: for behold, I bring you good tidings of great joy, which shall be to all people. For unto you is born this day in the city of David a Saviour, which is Christ the Lord. And this shall be a sign unto you; ye shall find the babe wrapped in swaddling clothes, lying in a manger." (Luke 2:8-12 KJV)

We notice in verse 8 that the shepherds were abiding in the "field" not "fields" as some translations say. Why *field*? Because these were not ordinary shepherds, but shepherd priests. Between Jerusalem and Bethlehem was a place called the Migdol Eder, meaning "Tower of the Flock." It was here where the sacrificial lambs that were to be used for the morning and evening sacrifices on the Temple Mount in

THE DNA OF JESUS CHRIST

Jerusalem were kept. It was here that the angel appeared unto these shepherd priests and not to ordinary shepherds. These priests would have understood the angel's proclamation due to their knowledge of the Scriptures regarding the coming Messiah, the Lamb of God, Jesus Christ. The message the angel gave them was of utmost importance: first, regarding the "sign" of swaddling clothes when they saw this baby; and secondly, His names announced to them by the angel. Swaddling clothes, Savior, Christ, Lord…what did it all mean? The angel's announcement let them know the "fullness of time" had come and Israel's Messiah was here.

When the shepherds went to see Jesus and saw Him wrapped in His swaddling clothing (death clothes), it confirmed the angel's message that He was the promised Messiah of Israel. There were two reasons they knew. First, according to the Scriptures in the Tenach (Old Testament)—which they knew by heart—their Messiah would be God come in the flesh, be born to die, be raised from the dead, ascend to heaven, and one day return to rule over the earth from Jerusalem, Israel, as prophesied in Isaiah 53, Psalm 22, Zechariah 12, and other scriptures. Second, this was confirmed by the angel in announcing Jesus' birth when he said, *"For unto you is born this day in the city of David, a "Saviour" which is "Christ" the "Lord."* "Saviour," meaning One who would give of His pure, sinless blood on the cross and deliver men and women from sin and death. "Christ," meaning "the anointed One" who would heal the sick, raise the dead, and work miracles. The "Lord," meaning He was God come in the flesh.

Another important point to remember is when the angel announced Jesus' birth to the shepherds, he did not say, "unto Mary is born this day," but "unto you is born this day." The wording of the angel demonstrates that this baby was sent not only to Mary but to Israel and the world as their Savior, Christ, and Lord.

Approximately two years after the birth of Jesus the Messiah, the wise men came from the East bearing gifts for Him of gold, frankincense, and myrrh. These were not gifts normally presented to a child but were very costly, signifying who Jesus was. The gold represented Jesus' royalty, for gold was brought before kings by their subjects. Frankincense represented His divinity and sweet smelling savor of His life's work to God the Father. Myrrh represented His suffering, death, and burial. The wise men's gifts revealed that Jesus was King, God, and Man. Therefore, the angel, shepherd priests, and wise men confirmed who Jesus was.

THE BRUISED HEEL
Although Jesus Christ was born to die for the sins of the world and to one day restore His entire creation back to a sinless environment, there would be a set time for Him to lay down His life and pour out His precious blood as the ultimate sacrifice. But Satan had other plans. From the time Jesus was born until His death on the cross, Satan tried to destroy Him through various means to get to His blood system as he had done with Adam and Eve, not knowing that it would be Jesus' volitional sacrifice and shed blood that would seal his doom forever.

Satan would enact His plans to destroy the Christ child, beginning with King Herod the Great, who was of the wicked seed of Satan. Herod had been visited by the wise men from the East, asking where they could find the one who had been born that was King of the Jews. It made the king furious, so he called in the chief priests and scribes, asking them where this Jewish King was to be born. They told him "Bethlehem," according to the Jewish prophet Micah (Micah 5:2). Herod then proceeded to have every male child, from two years and under in Bethlehem and the surrounding areas, killed in an attempt to destroy Jesus.

"Now when Jesus was born in Bethlehem of Judea in the days of Herod the king behold there came wise men from the east to Jerusalem, saying, Where is he that is born King of the Jews? for we have seen his star in the east, and are come to worship him. When Herod the king had heard these things, he was troubled, and all Jerusalem with him. And when Herod had gathered all the chief priests and scribes of the people together, he demanded of them where Christ should be born. And they said unto him, in Bethlehem of Judea: for thus it is written by the prophet, "And thou Bethlehem, in the land of Judah, art not the least among the princes of Judah: for out of thee, shall come a Governor, that shall rule my people Israel...Then Herod...sent forth, and slew all the children that were in Bethlehem, and in all the coasts thereof, from two years old and under, according to the time which he had diligently inquired of the wise men."
(Matthew 2:1-6, 16 KJV)

Before Herod had the babies killed, God warned Joseph in a dream to take Jesus and Mary and flee to Egypt until he was instructed by God to return to Israel. It is unknown exactly how long they were in Egypt, maybe two years; but after Herod died, they returned to Nazareth to live and raise Jesus.

THE TEMPTATIONS
Before Jesus began His ministry, He was led by the Holy Spirit into the wilderness to be tempted of the devil. It was during this forty day period that Satan tried to get to Jesus' blood system by having Him violate God's Word. The first way was to have Jesus turn the stones into bread; if Jesus had done so, He would have fulfilled His fleshly desire for food but it would have not been God's will at the time. It is interesting that food was the first temptation Satan put before Jesus, the same temptation which caused Adam and Eve to sin. Jesus used God's Word against Satan to overcome this temptation:

"Man shall not live by bread alone, but by every word that proceeds from the mouth of God." (Matthew 4:4 NKJ)

Satan then took Jesus to the Temple Mount and set Him on a pinnacle saying, "If you are the Son of God" jump off and the angels will catch you. It was another temptation to get the Lord Jesus to show who He was and gain public attention; but Satan also thought he could convince Jesus to kill Himself by committing suicide. This, too, would have been a sin:

"Then the devil taketh him up into the holy city, and setteth him on a pinnacle of the temple, and saith unto Him, If thou be the Son of God, cast thyself down: for it is written, He shall give his angels charge concerning thee: and in their hands they shall bear thee up, lest at any time thou dash thy foot against a stone. Jesus said unto him, It is

written again, Thou shalt not tempt the Lord thy God." (Matthew 4:5-7 KJV)

Satan told Jesus that if He would fall down and worship him, he would give Him the kingdoms of the world. Jesus would not do this because it would also have violated God's Word, for God only is to be worshipped.

"Again, the devil taketh him up into an exceeding high mountain, and sheweth him all the kingdoms of the world, and the glory of them; and saith unto him All these things will I give thee, if thou wilt fall down and worship me. Then saith Jesus unto him, Get thee hence, Satan: for it is written, Thou shalt worship the Lord thy God, and him only shalt thou serve." (Matthew 4:8-10 KJV)

Three times Satan tried to attack Jesus' blood system and thwart God's plan of redemption during His forty- day fast in the wilderness; however, each time Jesus overcame temptation by using God's Word against Satan.

Later, Satan would try to destroy Jesus again. In Nazareth, Jesus went into the synagogue on the Sabbath, read from the book of Isaiah, chapter 61 verses 1-2, and told the people He was fulfilling those Scriptures that day. Upon hearing that, along with the rest of His message, the people tried to throw Him off of a hill and kill Him (see Luke 4:16-30).

Satan tried again to destroy Jesus on the Temple Mount in Jerusalem when He confronted the Pharisees. They tried to stone Him to death, but He escaped out of their midst (see John 8:48-59).

All of these encounters were bringing Jesus closer and closer to His purpose on earth—to die on the cross. But why the cross? Why not some other method of death that was less cruel? To find the answer, we must go to the Old Testament where the cross is foreshadowed in types.

SIGNS OF THE CROSS
The CRUX
In Chapter 3, I explained how God created the sun, moon, and stars before He created man and used the stars as signs to be seen by humanity, revealing His plan of redemption. One of these signs is CRUX (The Cross) which, though "the smallest of 88 modern constellations, is one of the most distinctive."1 "The Hebrew name was Adom, which means *cutting off*, as in Daniel 9:26: "After threescore and two weeks shall Messiah be cut off." The Southern Cross was just visible in the latitude of Jerusalem at the time of the first coming of our Lord to die. Since then, through the gradual recession of the Polar Star, it has not been seen in northern latitudes. It gradually disappeared and became invisible at Jerusalem when the Real Sacrifice was offered there. It was not until the sixteenth century dawned that missionaries and voyagers, doubling the Cape for the first time and visiting the tropics and southern seas, brought back the news of "a wonderful cross more glorious than all the constellations of the heavens."2 This was the first sign of the cross, written in the stars before man was created, that told of a coming Redeemer who would die for the sins of the world.

Laminin
The second sign of the cross is most profound, in that it is found within man himself and has to do with the blood. It is

called Laminin, and it is the glue that holds us together. "Laminin is a protein that is part of the extracellular matrix in humans and animals. The extracellular matrix (ECM) lies outside of cells and provides support and attachment for cells inside organs (along with many other functions). Laminin has 'arms' that associate with other laminin molecules to form sheets and bind to cells. Laminin and other ECM proteins essentially 'glue' the cells (such as those lining the stomach and intestines) to a foundation of connective tissue. This keeps the cells in place and allows them to function properly. The structure of laminin is very important for its function (as is true for all proteins)."3 The beauty of laminin concerning God's creation of man is that it presents a picture in our blood system that points to the Cross of Calvary and our need for a Savior. The scriptures tell us that not only is Jesus Christ before all things (He is eternal), but by Him all things consist or hold together.

"For by him were all things created, that are in heaven, and that are in earth, visible and invisible, whether they be thrones, or dominions, or principalities, or powers: all things were created by him, and for him: And he is before all things, and by him all things consist (hold together)." (Colossians 1:16-17 KJV)

Tabernacle

The third sign of the cross is threefold and has to do with the Tabernacle in the Wilderness. God instructed Moses to build the Tabernacle after He delivered the Israelites from Egypt, as they were traveling through the wilderness to Canaan (known today as the land of Israel). The Tabernacle was the meeting place between God and Israel where the blood sacrifices were offered for inter-union and inter-communion between Him and His covenant people.

There were twelve tribes of Israel, and God instructed them to encamp around the Tabernacle according to their tribes. Three on the North: Naphtali, Asher, and Dan. Three on the East: Judah, Issachar, and Zebulun. Three on the West: Ephraim, Manasseh, and Benjamin. Three on the South: Gad, Simeon, and Reuben. If you had looked down on their encampment from above, you would have seen that it formed a cross with the Tabernacle inside. This cross is the first of the three having to do with the Tabernacle and the worship of God.

The second cross regarding the Tabernacle has to do with what I call the six stations of worship. Outside the Tabernacle enclosure was the Altar of Burnt Offering where the sacrifices were offered. Then there was the brazen laver which held the water for the priesthood to wash from before entering the Tabernacle itself. Inside, on the North wall, was the Table of Shewbread; on the South wall was the Seven Branch Golden Menorah; and on the West side, in front of a curtain that divided the Tabernacle into two parts—the Holy Place and the Most Holy Place (where God's Presence dwelt)—was the Golden Altar of Incense. Within the Most Holy Place were the Ark of the Covenant and the Mercy Seat. These six articles and the way they were positioned formed a cross.

The third cross regarding the Tabernacle had to do with the Shewbread (called Bread of the Face, or Bread of the Presence). These were twelve loaves of unleavened bread made from the finest wheat, representing each of the twelve tribes of Israel.

They were placed on the Golden Table of Shewbread and anointed in the middle with oil, in the form of a cross. Every aspect of the Tabernacle and its services pointed to Jesus Christ and His sacrificial death on the Cross. It all has to do with blood, DNA, blood covenanting, carrying forward the lineage of the godly seed of God's kingdom, and the defeat of Satan and his kingdom.

The Tav

The next sign of the cross in the Old Testament is in Ezekiel, chapter 9 and has to do with marking God's people. Many in Israel had turned away from God at the time and were worshipping idols; therefore, God was bringing judgment upon them. He sent six angels to Jerusalem to destroy the idol worshippers; but before they carried out God's instructions, He told the angels to put a mark on the foreheads of those who were still serving Him to protect them. That mark was a Tav, the last letter of the Hebrew alphabet, which at that time was written in the form of a cross (see Wikipedia on "Hebrew Alphabet"). It was the sign placed on the foreheads of the godly seed because of their true covenant relationship with God.

"And behold, six men (angels) came from the way of the higher gate, which lieth toward the north, and every man a slaughter weapon in his hand; and one man among them was clothed with linen, with a writer's inkhorn by his side: and they went in, and stood beside the brazen altar. And the glory of the God of Israel was gone up from the cherub, whereupon he was, to the threshold of the house. And he called to the man clothed with linen, which had the writer's inkhorn by his side; and the LORD said unto him, Go through the midst of the

city through the midst of Jerusalem, and set a mark upon the forehead of the men that sigh and that cry for all the abominations that be done in the midst thereof. And to the others he said in mine hearing, Go ye after him through the city, and smite: let not your eye spare, neither have ye pity: Slay utterly old and young, both maids, and little children, and women: but come not near any man upon whom is the mark (the cross); and begin at my sanctuary. Then they began at the ancient men which were before the house." (Ezekiel 9:2-6 KJV)

The "Tav" put a distinction between those who loved and served God and those who did not. This reminds us of the Book of Revelation, chapter 13, where in the last days, right before Jesus Christ returns and the Antichrist is ruling, people will be required to receive a mark on their hands and foreheads to show their loyalty to the Antichrist:

"And he (Antichrist) *causeth all, both small and great, rich and poor, free and bond, to receive a mark in their right hand, or in their foreheads: and that no man might buy or sell, save he that had the mark, or the name of the beast* (Antichrist), *or the number of his name."* (Revelation 13:16-17 KJV. Emphasis mine.)

In these last days, before the return of Christ, this mark will separate the seeds of Satan (ungodly people) from the godly seeds of God, for God's seeds (His people) will not take the mark.

"And the third angel followed them, saying with a loud voice, If any man worship the beast and his image, and receive his mark in his forehead, or in his hand, the same shall drink of the wine of the wrath of God, which is poured out without mixture into the cup of his

indignation; and he shall be tormented with fire and brimstone in the presence of the holy angels, and in the presence of the Lamb." (Revelation 14:9-10 KJV)

People who receive the mark of the Antichrist will seal their doom to an eternal hell; so make sure your life is hidden with Christ in God, *for when Christ, who is our life shall appear, then shall you also appear with Him in glory. (*Colossians 3:4 KJV)

Whirlpool Galaxy

The next sign of the cross is the Whirlpool Galaxy. The Whirlpool Galaxy is also known as Messier 51a—first seen by Charles Messier in 1773—and is a galaxy that we are the most familiar with. This galaxy, seen today through the Hubble Space Telescope, is located between 23 to 31 million light years away in the constellation Canes Venatici. Approximately 60 million light years across, its alignment to the earth is just about face-on, which gives us a great view not only of the galaxy but of its core. It can be seen with binoculars or a small telescope at night and found at the end of the handle of the Big Dipper. What is so amazing is when the Hubble Space Telescope zoomed to the center of this galaxy, it revealed a cross. Something else that I was drawn to was the red color in the circular pattern of the curving arms of the galaxy. This caused me to do some research to find out why it was such a dominant color, so I went to NASA's site regarding the Whirlpool Galaxy and was rather astounded at what I found. If you go to the following link, you will find these images by NASA's Hubble Space Telescope show off two dramatically different face-on views of the spiral galaxy M51, dubbed the Whirlpool Galaxy. Here is the web site.

www.hubblesite.org/newscenter
/archives/releases/2011/03.4

The red color of the curving arms of this galaxy, along with the cross in its center, is a reflection of Jesus' crucifixion and His blood that was shed for us. The Whirlpool Galaxy and the CRUX constellation were created by God before He created man, and both contain a picture of a cross as a sign of God's plan of redemption for His creation.

Washington D.C.

The last sign of the cross deals with our nation which was founded on the principles of God's Word. The Founding Fathers of the United States believed we were founded as a Christian nation. In fact the First Continental Congress opened with a Christian prayer, "O Lord our heavenly Father, high and mighty King of kings, and Lord of lords, who dost from thy throne behold all the dwellers of the earth and reignest with power supreme and uncontrolled over all the Kingdoms, Empires and Governments; look down in mercy, we beseech Thee on these our American States, who have fled to Thee from the rod of the oppressor and thrown themselves on Thy gracious protection, desiring to be henceforth dependent only on Thee." The prayer ended with "All this we ask **in the name and through the merits of Jesus Christ, Thy Son and our Savior. Amen.**" (Office of the Chaplin, U.S. House of Representatives.) The House Judiciary Committee, in 1854, stated that Christianity was the religion of the Founders of our republic.

The web site <u>CitizenLink.com</u> says that if we were to take a walk in Washington D.C., the path from the White House to the Washington Monument to the Lincoln Memorial to the Reflecting Pool to the Jefferson Memorial to the Smithsonian to the Capitol and back to the White House forms a cross. Also, each one of the Memorials has an inscription referring to God, some with scriptures. All of this can be found right in the center of our nation's government, a government that has continued to turn away from God. Unless we repent as a nation, God's hand of judgment is going to fall on the United States.

SACRIFICIAL BLOOD
This brings us to the reason for Jesus' coming to earth: His crucifixion.

During Jesus' ministry, He continually destroyed the works of Satan by healing the sick, raising the dead, casting out devils, and teaching God's Word to the multitudes. Now the time had come which had been planned before the world was framed, to offer Himself as a blood covenant sacrifice in Jerusalem, Israel, and make a way for those who would believe in and serve Him to come into a covenant relationship with Him.

The many prophecies of the Old Testament of a Coming Messiah were about to be fulfilled. After over 4,000 years of waiting, God's plan of redemption was now to be implemented. The stage was set, all the characters were in place, and the curtain was coming up on the main act. The precious, sinless, life-giving blood that flowed through Jesus' body was now to be poured out as the Sacrifice Lamb.

Crucifixion was the cruelest of deaths, but it had to be this way; for as the sacrificial animal was slain to get to its life—for life is in the blood—even so would Jesus have to be slain to bring forth His blood that man might be freed from sin, death, and hell. His shed blood held the key that would redeem His creation, carry forth the spiritual lineage of the godly seed, and birth many spiritual sons and daughters into the kingdom of God. The Paramount Battle of Genesis 3:15 was now underway as Satan and his seeds (evil men) began to bruise the heel of the Seed (Jesus) of the woman (Eve).

Jerusalem, Israel, was the stage because it was the place of the Temple, the priesthood, and the sacrificial system that allowed the Jewish people to be in inter-union and inter-communion with God. It is the place God chose as His Covenant City and where Jesus had to die, be resurrected, and ascend to heaven. It is the city where He will one day soon return, establish His kingdom on earth, and rule the nations.

The events leading to the Crucifixion happened little by little. It began at the Passover Meal, as Jesus sat at the table with His disciples and instituted the Lord's Supper. Judas, His betrayer, sat beside Him but was about to fulfill his mission by leading the Temple guards to Jesus in the Garden of Gethsemane:

"When the hour had come, He sat down, and the twelve apostles with Him. Then He said to them "With desire I have desired to eat this Passover with you before I suffer; for I say to you, I will no longer eat

of it until it is fulfilled in the kingdom of God...And He took the bread, gave thanks and broke it and gave it to them, saying, "This is My body which is given for you; do this in remembrance of Me." Likewise He took the cup after supper, saying, "This cup is the new covenant in My blood, which is shed for you." But behold, the hand of My betrayer is with Me on the table. And truly the Son of Man goes as it has been determined, but woe to that man by whom He is betrayed!" (Luke 22:14-22 NKJ)

The Passover Lamb and its blood, which had saved Israel's firstborn when the death angel passed over Egypt, was now going to be fulfilled in the true Passover Lamb, Jesus Christ, who would defeat death and give eternal life to those who believe in and serve Him.

After supper, Jesus and His remaining disciples went to the Garden of Gethsemane (which means "wine press"). It was in this garden that the Lord Jesus would experience such mental anguish regarding His coming crucifixion that His capillaries burst and the blood came to the surface of His skin as great drops. Redemption had begun.

From the garden, Jesus was taken by the guard to the palace of Annas for interrogation, then to Caiaphus and the Sanhedrin, then to Pilate, then King Herod Antipas, then back to Pilate, and finally to the cross. There was the spitting, the slapping, the rod, the scourging, the crown of thorns, the cross, the nails, and the spear. The pure, sinless blood of Jesus Christ came forth; now it was spurting, running, and pouring forth upon His body and the earth. The Fountain of Life had been tapped and was coming forth for sinful man.

There were cries of pain and agony, His bones showing; there was spit, sweat, dirt, clotted and dried blood, His mangled flesh, and His thirst. The One who made the oceans, lakes, and rivers cried out for a drink of water; below Him were His disciples and His heartbroken mother. The blood flowed, dripped, and spurted as the spirits of darkness, driving evil men, continued to taunt, *"If thou be the Son of God, come down from the cross."* (Matthew 27:40 KJV)

Then Jesus said, "It is finished!" Suddenly things started to happen. The earth began to quake and tremble, the sun was darkened, and the veil in the Temple was rent from top to bottom. The "crushing of the Serpent's head (Satan)" had begun with the first drop of Jesus' blood being shed. Now the "Champion of God," the "Seed of the woman, (Jesus)" met the champion of the seed of evil (Satan) in the spirit world face-to-face, in the presence of Satan's forces, the angels of God, all of heaven, and God the Father. They had all watched one single Man take on the full strength of Satan's power, and now they watched as the Son of God made an open spectacle of him. Jesus' Resurrection would not come for three days, but the battle had been won:

"Having spoiled principalities and powers, he made a shew of them openly, triumphing over them in it (the cross)." (Colossians 2:15 KJV. Emphasis mine.)

"Forasmuch then as the children are partakers of flesh and blood, he also himself likewise took part of the same; that through death he might destroy him that had the power of death, that is, the devil; and

deliver them who through fear of death were all their lifetime subject to bondage." (Hebrews 2:14-15 KJV)

Redemption was forever sealed. God the Son had become a man, given His life, and made a way for all who would, to be saved. Nature, the earth, and the universe will later be restored to perfection. Satan and his kingdom of darkness, rebellion, sin, and hate had been defeated and would one day be done away with forever. Three days after Jesus' Crucifixion, the greatest event in human history would take place—Jesus would rise from the dead in a glorified body. Others had come back from the dead, such as Lazarus and the son of the widow woman from Nain, only to die again and their bodies return to the dust; but Jesus Christ was alive forevermore. Through His Resurrection, Jesus' spiritual DNA would be passed on to many generations through *the new birth experience* or *being born again*. His death and resurrection would reverberate around the world, century after century, changing the lives of multitudes for all eternity.

Chapter 9
WAS HE REAL AND DID HE DIE?

"Joseph of Arimathea...went to Pilate, and asked for the body of Jesus.
Pilate marveled that He was already dead; and summoning the
centurion, he asked him if He had been dead for some time. So when
he found out from the centurion, he granted the body to Joseph."
(Mark 15:43-45 NKJ)

Much has been made of Jesus Christ through the centuries, and many have tried to disprove that He was a historical figure. Others have agreed that He was a real person and that He was crucified, but He did not really die. Since Christianity stands or falls on the crucifixion, death, and Resurrection of Jesus Christ, I am going to deal with two of these issues now: the historicity and the crucifixion and death of Jesus. In the next chapter we will deal with His Resurrection.

JESUS CHRIST, A REAL HISTORICAL FIGURE
Anyone who is a historical scholar or has studied history relating to Jesus Christ knows that He was a true historical figure. There are many non-biblical sources regarding His historicity, as well as the writings of the early church fathers. There is also the absolute reliability of the New Testament documents showing Jesus Christ to be a real person in history.

"As F. F. Bruce, Ryland's professor of biblical criticism and exegesis at the University of Manchester has rightly said: 'Some writers may toy with the fancy of a "Christ-myth," but they do not do so on the ground of historical evidence. The historicity of Christ is as axiomatic for an unbiased historian as the historicity of Julius Caesar. It is not historians who propagate the "Christ-myth" theories."[1]

NON-BIBLICAL SOURCES FOR JESUS' HISTORICITY
Flavius Josephus

Josephus was born in 37 A.D. and was the commander of the Jewish forces in Galilee. He was captured by the Romans but, based on a divine revelation he claimed to have concerning Vespasian becoming emperor of Rome, was released when his prophecy came true. He went to Rome and became a Roman citizen. It was there that he wrote, *War of the Jews* and *Antiquities of the Jews*, the latter being an extra-biblical account of Jewish history from the period of the Maccabees to the destruction of Jerusalem and Its Temple. In his writings he spoke of Herod the Great, Pontius Pilate, John the Baptist, and Jesus Christ.

"In a passage in *Antiquities*, 18.3.3: He says of Jesus Christ, 'Now there was about this time Jesus, a wise man...This man was the Christ. And when Pilate had condemned him to the cross, upon his impeachment by the principal man among us, those he had loved from the first did not forsake him, for he appeared to them alive on the third day'..."[2]

Some have tried to disprove that Josephus wrote this, but it was used by Eusebius in the fourth century and "is reiterated by the most recent Loeb edition of his works. And it is all the more remarkable when we remember that, so far from being sympathetic to Christians, Josephus was a Jew writing to please the Romans. This story would not have pleased them in the slightest. He would hardly have included it if it were not true."3

Cornelius Tacitus

Cornelius Tacitus was born somewhere between A.D. 52 and 54; he was a Roman citizen as well as a historian. He wrote of the reign of Nero and of Nero's setting fire to Rome, blaming the Christians, who, Tacitus said, were followers of Christus (Christ) who had been put to death by Pontius Pilate.

Letter of Mara Bar-Sereapion

F.F. Bruce (*The New Testament Documents: Are They Reliable?*) Used by permission of Inter-Varsity Press, Downers Grove, ILL.) records that there is "...in the British Museum an interesting manuscript preserving the text of a letter written some time later than A.D. 73...This letter was sent by a Syrian named Mara Bar-Serapion to his son Serapion. Mara Bar-Serapion was in prison at the time, but he wrote to encourage his son in the pursuit of wisdom, and pointed out that those who persecuted wise men were overtaken by misfortune. He instances the deaths of Socrates, Pythagoras and Christ."4

Plinius Secundus

In 112 A.D., Pliny the Younger was the governor of Bithynia. In writing to the emperor Trajan, he spoke of killing Christians, stating that many of them would not bow down to a statue of Trajan but were committed to Christ, believing that Jesus was a god.

These are just a few of the non-biblical writers who confirmed Jesus was a real historical figure. Others are Tertullian, Thallus, Seutonius, Lucian, and also the Jewish Talmud which speak of Jesus Christ in a derogatory manner.

BIBLICAL SOURCES FOR JESUS' HISTORICITY
Polycarp
Polycarp lived between 70 and 156 A.D. and was a disciple of the apostle John. He served as the bishop of the church at Smyrna and was a major combatant against heresies regarding Christianity. He was martyred at the age of 86 by the Roman government by being burned alive at the stake. He died because of his unyielding faith in Jesus Christ. His life and martyrdom are verifiable, historical facts.

Origen
Origen was born in 184 or 185 A.D. in Alexandria, Egypt, and was raised in a Christian home. His father, Leonides, taught him the Scriptures. He had a brilliant mind and, as a young boy, memorized large portions of the Bible. He was fiercely loyal to Jesus Christ and an avid combatant of heresies. He compiled the *Hexapla*, which was an edition of the Bible containing the Hebrew text and five Greek translations. He wrote many books, the most important being *De Principils* which dealt with systematic theology. He moved to Caesarea where he remained until his death.

Irenaeus
Irenaeus was born to Greek parents around 125 A.D. and died in 202 A.D. His writings gave him a prominent place among the Church fathers and were the foundation stones of Christian

theology, exposing and refuting the errors of false doctrine. As a child, he saw and heard Polycarp who studied under the apostle John. "According to tradition, the Apostle John, as a very old man who had 'seen the Lord' (i.e., Jesus), lived at Ephesus in the days when Polycarp was young. Thus, there were three generations between Jesus of Nazareth and Irenaeus of southern France."5

There were other biblical writers who wrote of Jesus' historicity, such as Justin Martyr, Eusebius, Ignatius, Tertullian, Jerome, St. Clement of Rome, and St. Athanasius. These all confirm Jesus to be a real person; however, our greatest proof is the Old Testament with its 300 prophecies of a coming Messiah and the New Testament, which shows how Jesus Christ fulfilled each of these in every detail.

JESUS CHRIST'S CRUCIFIXION AND DEATH
Now that we have given evidence of Jesus' history, we turn to His crucifixion and death; we will use historical and biblical accounts to verify these two events.

CRUCIFIXION
Crucifixion was the cruelest of deaths. In Jesus' case, He was taken before Pilate who interrogated him before sending Him to be scourged and crucified. The Roman soldiers first whipped Him with a flagrum, which consisted of three separate thongs, each with two lead balls at the end, giving added weight to the whip and causing major damage to the victim, even to the point of exposing the veins and sometimes the internal organs. Once scourged, Jesus was taken to be crucified: *"And when he*

had scourged Jesus, he delivered him to be crucified." (Matthew 27:26 NKJ)

On the way to Golgotha (the place of crucifixion) Jesus was forced to carry the patibulum, a horizontal piece of the cross weighing 70 to 100 pounds. Being so weak from lack of sleep and food and the scourging, He fell beneath the weight. The Roman soldiers made a man by the name of Simon of Cyrene carry it the rest of the way.

"And as they came out, they found a man of Cyrene, Simon by name: him they compelled to bear his cross. And when they were come unto a place called Golgotha, that is to say, a place of a skull...they crucified him, and parted his garments casting lots, that it might be fulfilled which was spoken by the prophet (Psalm 22:18), They parted my garments among them, and upon my vesture did they cast lots." (Matthew 27:32-33, 35 KJV)

The suffering of a crucifixion victim was horrendous. "The unnatural position made every movement painful; the lacerated veins and crushed tendons throbbed with incessant anguish; the wounds, inflamed by exposure, gradually gangrened; the arteries—especially at the head and stomach— became swollen and oppressed with surcharged blood; and while each variety of misery went on gradually increasing, there was added to them the intolerable pang of a burning and raging thirst."6

Because it was a Jewish high holy day, the Jewish leaders asked Pilate to have the crucified victims' bodies taken down before sunset, which Pilate agreed to do. To speed up the death process, the Roman soldiers broke the legs of the victims to further hinder their breathing. When the soldiers came to Jesus, He was already dead, so they did not break His bones, which fulfilled Psalm 34:20. Seeing that Jesus was dead, a Roman soldier pierced His side with a spear which brought forth blood and water, another sign He was dead.

"The Jews therefore, because it was the preparation, that the bodies should not remain upon the cross on the sabbath day, (for the sabbath day was an high day), besought Pilate that their legs might be broken, and that they might be taken away. Then came the soldiers, and brake the legs of the first, and of the other which was crucified with him. But when they came to Jesus, and saw that he was dead already, they brake not his legs: But one of the soldiers with a spear pierced his side, and forthwith came there out blood and water." (John 19:31-34 KJV)

In writing of Christ's death, Michael Green explains: "We are told on eyewitness authority that 'blood and water' came out of the pierced side of Jesus. The eyewitness clearly attached great importance to this. Had Jesus been alive when the spear pierced his side, strong spouts of blood would have emerged with every heart beat. Instead, the observer noticed semi-solid dark serum. This is evidence of massive clotting of the blood in the main arteries, and is exceptionally strong proof of death. It is all the more impressive because the evangelist could not possibly have realized its significance to a pathologist. The 'blood and water' from the spear-thrust is proof positive that Jesus was already dead."7

When Joseph of Arimathea went to Pilate to ask for the body of Jesus, Pilate asked for certification that Jesus was dead. Four executioners had examined Him to confirm His death before Joseph went to Pilate. Therefore Jesus was absolutely dead.

"Joseph of Arimathea, a prominent council member (member of the Sanhedrin), *who was himself waiting for the kingdom of God coming and taking courage, went in to Pilate and asked for the body of Jesus. Pilate marveled that He was already dead; and summoning the centurion, he asked him if He had been dead for some time. So when he found out from the centurion, he granted the body to Joseph."* (Mark 15:43-45 NKJ. Emphasis mine.)

These accounts completely confirm Jesus was dead when He was taken to the tomb to be buried. This does not take into account the preparation for His burial which included Jesus being wrapped in linen cloth and the application of about 100 pounds of myrrh and aloes which sealed His body inside the wrappings. No one could survive that.

SHROUD OF TURIN

Although much has been made of the Shroud of Turin, about whether or not it is the burial cloth of Jesus Christ, new evidence reveals that the blood areas on the Shroud are real blood stains (Type AB, which is the rarest blood group) and not artistic pigments. "A medieval artist would have needed a thorough knowledge of "'light negativity, light spectometry, microscopy, radiology, human physiology, pathology, hematology, endocrinology, forensic and archaeology' in order to create such a sophisticated image."8 Also, no brush strokes or paint pigment have ever been found on the cloth.

"Whatever the mechanism was that created the image, it operated uniformly over the entire body and 'encoded' the presence of different types of organic material, such as skin and hair. Furthermore, the image was formed in vertical, straight-line paths, as if every pore and every hair of the body contained a microminiature laser."9

"Dr. Robert Bucklin, deputy coroner and forensic pathologist at the Los Angeles County Hospital gives his expert reading of the negatives of the Man on the Shroud...*Irrespective of how the images were made, there is adequate information here to state that they are anatomically correct. There is no problem in diagnosing what happened to this individual. The pathology and physiology are unquestionable and represent medical knowledge unknown 150 years ago. This is a 5-foot, 11-inch male Caucasian weighing about 178 pounds. The lesions are as follows: beginning at the head, there are blood flows from numerous puncture wounds on the top and back of the scalp and forehead. The man has been beaten about the face, there is a swelling over one cheek, and he undoubtedly has a black eye. His nose tip is abraded, as would occur from a fall, and it appears that the nasal cartilage may have separated from the bone. There is a wound in the left wrist, the right one being covered by the left hand. This is the typical lesion of a crucifixion.*

There is a stream of blood down both arms. Here and there, there are blood drips at an angle from the main blood flow in response to gravity. These angles represent the only ones that can occur from the only two positions which can be taken by a body during crucifixion. On the back and on the front there are lesions which appear to be scourge marks. Historians have indicated that Romans used a whip called a flagrum. This whip had two or three thongs, and at their ends there were pieces of metal or bone which look like small dumbbells. These were designed to gouge out flesh. The thongs and metal end-pieces from a Roman flagrum fit precisely into the anterior and posterior scourge lesions on the body. The victim was whipped from both sides by two men, one of whom was taller than the other, as demonstrated by the angle of the thongs.

*There is a swelling of both shoulders, with abrasions indicating that something heavy and rough had been carried across the man's shoulders within hours of death. On the right flank, a long, narrow blade of some type entered in an upward direction, pierced the diaphragm, penetrated into the thoracic cavity through the lung into the heart. This was a post-mortem event, because separate components of red cells and clear serum drained from the lesion. Later, after the corpse was laid out horizontally and face up on the cloth, blood dribbled out of the side wound and puddled along the small of the back. There is no evidence of either leg being fractured. There is an abrasion of one knee, commensurate with a fall (as is the abraded nose tip); and, finally, a spike had been driven through both feet, and blood had leaked from both wounds onto the cloth. The evidence of a scourged man who was crucified and died from the cardiopulmonary failure typical of crucifixion is clear-cut."*10

As stated before, the blood has been analyzed and is Type AB, the rarest of blood type groups. **This does not mean that Jesus' blood and DNA came from a human source. For as Adam's blood came from God, so did Jesus'.** That is why He was sinless, and His pure, sinless blood could redeem mankind from the curse of sin.

The 1988 carbon dating of the Shroud has proven to be incorrect (see "Shroud of Turin" website). Therefore, with the accumulated evidence at hand, we can come to a conclusive determination that if this is the Shroud of Jesus Christ, He was indeed crucified to death.

Below is a list of only ten of the Old Testament prophetic Scriptures fulfilled by Jesus regarding His crucifixion and death. The odds for one man to fulfill just eight of these is 1 to the 17th power.

TEN PROPHETIC SCRIPTURES FULFILLED REGARDING JESUS' DEATH:
Betrayed for 30 pieces of silver: Zechariah 11:12, fulfilled in Matthew 27:26.
Accused by false witnesses: Psalm 35:11, fulfilled in Matthew 26:59-61.
Wounded and bruised: Isaiah 53:5, fulfilled in Matthew 27:26.
Smitten and spat upon: Isaiah 50:6, fulfilled in Matthew 26:67.
Hands and feet pierced: Psalm 22:16, fulfilled in Luke 23:33.
Garments parted and lots cast for them: Psalm 22:18, fulfilled in John 19:23, 24.
Gall and vinegar offered Him: Psalm 69:21, fulfilled in Matthew 27:34.
Bones not broken: Psalm 34:20, fulfilled in John 19:33.
Side pierced: Zechariah 12:10, fulfilled in John 19:34.
Buried in a rich man's tomb: Isaiah 53:9, fulfilled in Matthew 27:57-60.

After Jesus' Crucifixion, He rose from the dead, appeared to many, and through the preaching of His disciples, thousands of

Jews in Jerusalem accepted Him as their Savior and Messiah. This brings us to the subject of the Resurrection and the evidence to support this unprecedented event.

Chapter 10
THE RESURRECTION

"And the angel answered and said unto the women, Fear not ye: for I know that ye seek Jesus, which was crucified. He is not here: for he is risen, as he said. Come, see the place where the Lord lay. And go quickly, and tell his disciples that he is risen from the dead; and, behold, he goeth before you into Galilee; there shall ye see him; lo, I have told you." (Matthew 28:5-7 KJV)

If a friend of yours told you he was going to die at a certain time, then after three days rise from the dead, you would undoubtedly think he was somewhat looney and needed help, right? Only a fool would say something like that unless he knew for sure it was going to happen. There has never been a person in the entire world who was able to make that statement and fulfill it except One—Jesus Christ. Not only did He tell His disciples He would rise from the dead, but He also told the religious leaders of Israel. It happened just as He said and turned the world upside down.

Down through the centuries, many have tried to disprove the Resurrection of Jesus Christ; therefore, since Christianity stands and falls on this issue, let us examine the evidence so we can decide for ourselves.

JESUS' CLAIMS OF HIS RESURRECTION
As we examine the biblical text, we find that Jesus spoke of His Resurrection several times:

"From that time forth began Jesus to show unto his disciples, how that he must go unto Jerusalem, and suffer many things of the elders and chief priests and scribes, and be killed, and be raised again the third day." (Matthew 16:21 KJV)

"And Jesus going up to Jerusalem took the twelve disciples apart in the way, and said unto them, Behold we go up to Jerusalem; and the Son of man shall be betrayed unto the chief priests and unto the scribes, and they shall condemn him to death, and shall deliver him to the Gentiles to mock, and to scourge, and to crucify him: and the third day he shall rise again." (Matthew 20:17-19, KJV.) *"But after that I am risen, I will go before you into Galilee."* (Mark 14:28 KJV)

After Jesus' burial, the Jewish leaders asked that the Roman seal be placed on the huge stone covering the entrance to the tomb (the Seal was a sign of authentication and proof that the tomb was occupied) and a Roman guard placed there in case his disciples tried to steal His body. The following Scriptures tell the story:

"Now the next day, that followed the day of the preparation, the chief priests and Pharisees came together unto Pilate, saying, Sir, we remember that that deceiver said, while he was yet alive, After three days I will rise again. Command therefore that the sepulchre be made sure until the third day, lest his disciples come by night, and steal him away, and say unto the people, He is risen from the dead: so the last error shall be worse than the first. Pilate said unto them, Ye have a watch: go your way, make it as sure as ye can. So they went, and made the sepulchre sure, sealing the stone, and setting a watch." (Matthew 27:62-66 KJV)

There are several things of utmost importance in these Scriptures. First, the Jewish leaders knew without a doubt that Jesus was dead. Second, they were really concerned that He might rise from the dead as He had said. Third, the stone at the tomb's entrance was so large it took several men to move it. Fourth, the tomb was made secure with a Roman seal; anyone who broke the seal would suffer an unpleasant death. Fifth, the Roman guard consisted of sixteen Roman soldiers, each of which was responsible for six square feet of space. If a guard fell asleep while on duty, he was killed along with the other fifteen.

As far as Jesus' disciples stealing His body was concerned, they were so terrified after Jesus' death that they all hid somewhere; and we do not hear anything else about them until the women who had gone to the tomb and found it empty came and told them.

JESUS' RESURRECTION
The Bible tells us when Jesus rose from the dead there was a great earthquake, the large stone was moved away by an angel, and His grave clothes were lying on the stone slab where His body had been. When the Roman guards saw the angel, they were filled with fear, shook, and fell to the ground as dead men. After they recovered from being knocked to the ground by the power of God, they went to the Jewish leaders and told them all that had happened. The Jewish leaders gave them a large sum of money and told them to say Jesus' disciples came by night and stole His body. If the news reached Pilate's ears, they would defend the guards.

This was a preposterous plan, for the Jewish leaders knew, according to Roman law, if the Roman guards had fallen asleep and allowed the disciples to steal Jesus' body, they would be put to death. Also, they could not explain the guards being filled with fear and knocked to the ground after seeing an angel descend from heaven and move the stone away. Roman soldiers were the most fearless of men, but what they experienced was a highly unusual event. The following scriptures verify what happened:

"And, behold, there was a great earthquake: for an angel of the Lord descended from heaven, and came and rolled back the stone from the door, and sat on it. His countenance was like lightning and his clothing as white as snow: And the guards shook for fear of him, and became like dead men. But the angel answered and said to the women, do not be afraid, for I know that you seek Jesus, who was crucified. He is not here: for he is risen, as he said. Come, see the place where the Lord lay. And go quickly, and tell his disciples that he is risen from the dead...Now while they were going, behold, some of the guard came into the city and reported to the chief priests all the things that had happened. When they had assembled with the elders and consulted together, they gave a large sum of money to the soldiers, saying, "Tell them, 'His disciples came at night and stole Him away while we slept.' And if this comes to the governor's ears, we will appease him and make you secure." (Matthew 28:2-7, 11-14 NKJ)

Later, the Jewish apostle Peter stood on the Temple Mount in Jerusalem and preached that dynamic message of Jesus' Resurrection. It was on the Day of Pentecost, right after the Holy Spirit descended from heaven and filled the disciples, causing them to speak in other tongues. The people thought they were drunk, but Peter corrected them and began to preach:

"Men of Israel, hear these words: Jesus of Nazareth, a Man attested by God to you by miracles, wonders, and signs which God did through Him in your midst, as you yourselves also know—Him, being delivered by the determined purpose and foreknowledge of God, you have taken by lawless hands, have crucified, and put to death; whom God raised up, having loosed the pains of death, because it was not possible that He should be held by it. For David says concerning Him: 'I foresaw the LORD always before my face, for He is at my right hand, that I may not be shaken. Therefore my heart rejoiced, and my tongue was glad; moreover my flesh also will rest in hope. For You will not leave my soul in Hades, nor will You allow Your Holy One to see corruption. You have made know to me the ways of life; You will make me full of joy in Your presence.' "Men and brethren, let me speak freely to you of the patriarch David, that he is both dead and buried, and his tomb is with us to this day. Therefore, being a prophet, and knowing that God had sworn with an oath to him that of the fruit of his body, according to the flesh, He would raise up the Christ to sit on his throne, he, foreseeing this, spoke concerning the resurrection of the Christ, that His soul was not left in Hades, nor did His flesh see corruption. This Jesus God has raised up, of which we are all witnesses. Therefore, being exalted to the right hand of God and having received from the Father the promise of the Holy Spirit, He poured out this which you now see and hear. For David did not ascend into the heavens, but he says himself: 'The LORD said to my Lord, "Sit at My right hand, till I make Your enemies Your footstool." Therefore, let all the house of Israel know assuredly that God has made this Jesus, whom you crucified, both Lord and Christ."
(Acts 2:22-36 NKJ)

Peter confronted the religious leaders with the truth of Jesus' Resurrection and they could not refute it. Probably everyone in Jerusalem knew the tomb was empty and Jesus had truly risen from the dead. Jesus' Resurrection was the reason for the Holy Spirit's outpouring, plus it validated His Messianic Kingly position as the heir to the throne of David. Due to Peter's sermon, that day 3,000 Jewish souls believed that Jesus was their Messiah; they were saved and baptized in water.

How the Resurrection of Jesus took place, we do not know for sure, but Dr. Richard Kent, on his Web Site, www.freechristianteaching.org, gives a compelling account of what could have happened in his article 7, "The Shroud of Turin and Jesus' Resurrection":

SHROUD OF TURIN AND JESUS' RESURRECTION
"We believe that X-rays were probably released at the Resurrection, caused by the intense radiation of light and subatomic particles, moving at the speed of light, interacting with the linen of the Shroud.

We believe that the effect of the radiation of light and subatomic particles emitted at the Resurrection was similar to a confined nuclear reaction, with the generation of soft X-rays.

Many observers have commented that the image on the Shroud is fundamentally similar to an X-ray. This observation may be very accurate.[1]

The first photograph of the Shroud in 1898

Interest in the Shroud...dramatically increased in 1898 when the Italian photographer Secundo Pla took the first photograph of the Shroud in 1898. Both pictures below have a mixture of photo-positive and photo-negative images, which we will study in detail.

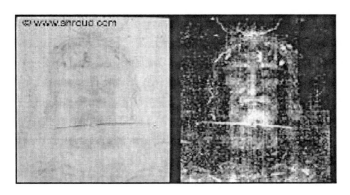

*The picture on the above left is a photo-positive of the face on the Shroud, with red blood marks from the Crown of Thorns. There is a faint image of a face, which is in photo-negative, making it difficult to understand.*2

To Secundo Pla's astonishment the photo-negative face image on the Shroud (above left) became a photo-positive image on his camera negative (above right), except that the blood was in photo-negative, and therefore appears white on the black and white negative. The image of the Crucified Man in the photo-positive is now much more clearly seen!

The blood stains on the Shroud

The Shroud has blood marks on the scalp, both wrists, the right chest wall, and both ankles. This photograph of the Shroud clearly shows blood marks (in white) over the scalp, both wrists (with blood flows from both puncture wounds), blood flows from both plantar surfaces of the feet (see the dorsal image below right), and multiple laceration wounds from the Scourging. The blood has been analyzed. It is Type AB, the rarest blood group, and also contains a high level of Bilirubin. This is a bile pigment, which is found in high levels in blood of torture victims. The bile pigment Bilirubin is bright red. This red color is maintained post mortem, and accounts for the bright coloration of the blood on the Shroud (**As I said before, if the blood on the Shroud is Jesus Christ's, it does not mean His blood, or DNA, came from a human source. The first man, Adam, did not receive his blood and DNA from a human source, neither did Jesus Christ, regardless of what their blood types were. They both came from God. It is a moot point**).

Dr. Accetta's experiment confirms radiation

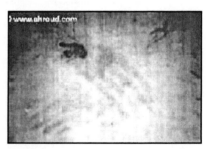

The X-ray effect has been duplicated by Dr. Accetta's experiment. Dr. Accetta injected himself with a radioactive material and stood in front of a VP8 Image Analyzing computer. The results are very interesting, and certainly demonstrate the mechanism of the Image on the Shroud involved radiation.

The X-ray appearance of the anatomical hands on the Shroud

The X-ray effect is certainly given added credibility by the hands on the Shroud, which appear to be an X-ray of the underlying metacarpal bones and phalanges of Jesus Christ hands."[3]

Dr. Richard Kent gives details of Jesus' appearances on his web site www.freechristianteaching.org article 6 on "the Shroud of Turin and Jesus' Resurrection." He lists 7 different physical aspects of Jesus' Body while on earth after His Resurrection:

Jesus' post-Resurrection appearances

1. *He still bore the marks of the wounds in His hands, feet, and chest wall (John 20:20).*
2. *He could be seen and touched as a physical Body of flesh and bones (Matthew 28:9, Luke 24:37-39).*
3. *He invited people to examine His body (Luke 24:39-40, John 20:20, 27).*
4. *Jesus ate and drank with His disciples after His Resurrection (Luke 24:41-43; Acts 10:41).*
5. *Jesus could appear and disappear in a closed room, indicating that He was not confined to the normal physical laws of time and space.*
6. *After His Resurrection, Jesus Christ appeared to Mary Magdalene by the Tomb (John 20:10-18), Mary and the other women (Matthew 28:1-10), Peter (I Corinthians 15:5), two disciples on the road to Emmaus (Luke 24:13-35), ten disciples (Luke 24:36-49), eleven disciples in a room (John 20:24-31), seven disciples by the Sea of Galilee (John 21), all the disciples (Matthew 28:16-20), five hundred people (I Corinthians 15:6), James (I Corinthians 15:7), all the disciples again before He ascended to Heaven (Acts 1:4-8), accompanied by two men in white clothes (possibly Moses and Elijah), and to Saul on his way to Damascus (Acts 9:1-9) who became Paul.*
7. *In other words, Jesus Christ appears to have been living outside the fourth dimension, Time."*4

The Resurrection of Jesus Christ is factual and no person, having once studied the evidence in an unbiased manner, can say otherwise.

TESTIMONIES OF HIGHLY INFLUENTIAL MEN

Lord Lyndhurst was born in 1772 and died in 1863. He was "recognized as one of the greatest legal minds in British history, the Solicitor-General of the British government in 1819, attorney-general of Great Britain in 1824, three times High Chancellor of England, and elected in 1846, High Steward of the University of Cambridge, thus holding in one lifetime the highest offices which a judge in Great Britain could ever have conferred upon him. When Chancellor Lyndhurst died, a document was found in his desk, among his private papers, giving an extended account of his own Christian faith, and in this precious previously unknown record, he wrote: 'I know pretty well what evidence is and I tell you, such evidence as that for the Resurrection has never broken down yet.'"[5]

- *"Clifford Herschel Moore*, professor at Harvard University, well said, 'Christianity knew its Saviour and Redeemer not as some god whose history was contained in a mythical faith, with rude, primitive, and even offensive elements...Jesus was a historical not a mythical being. No remote or foul myth obtruded itself of the Christian believer; his faith was founded on positive, historical, and acceptable facts.'"[6]

JESUS' BODY DID NOT SEE CORRUPTION

Since God created the universe and everything in it, there is no reason to believe that He could not raise Jesus from the dead.

Jesus Christ's body did not see corruption (decay) as have others who have died, but He was resurrected in three days with a glorified body. The Apostle Peter spoke of Jesus' body not seeing corruption in his sermon on the day of Pentecost:

"Because thou wilt not leave my soul in hell, neither wilt thou suffer thine Holy One to see corruption." (Acts 2:27 KJV)

The Apostle Paul also quoted the same Scripture in his message in the synagogue in Antioch, in Acts 13:35.

In concluding this chapter on the Resurrection of Jesus Christ, I want to say that our future rests on this truth. For those who believe, make Jesus Christ Savior and Lord of their lives, pray, study the Scriptures, and are obedient to Him, there are great rewards here on earth. I am not talking about finances, although God may bless us with that; I am referring to the peace, joy, and fulfillment that come in serving Him—plus the reward of an eternal life in Heaven after we die.

For those who do not believe, it is not due to lack of evidence but a willful rejecting of the truth in order to live their lives the way they want. The end of such a life is one of eternal torment in the Lake of Fire.

The next chapter will give a clear understanding of our makeup as humans, the reason for our being on earth, how Jesus' Resurrection applies to our lives, and how to secure our future.

Chapter 11
YOUR ETERNAL DESTINY

"And I saw the dead, small and great, stand before God; and the books were opened: and another book was opened which is the book of life: and the dead were judged out of those things which were written in the books, according to their works. And whosoever was not found written in the book of life, was cast into the lake of fire." (Revelation 20:12, 15 KJV)

Death! It is a word that puts fear in most people because of the unknown; but what about death? How does it feel to die, is there life after death, and, if so, what kind of life is it? Where do we go when we die? Is this life on earth all there is? Do we just float around somewhere, or do we become reincarnated into someone or something else? Is there really such a thing as a resurrection from the dead? These are valid questions, but can we find real answers anywhere? Thankfully we can, in both the Bible and contemporary accounts.

Before we answer these questions, I feel it is necessary to lay some groundwork for those who may know nothing about the three parts of our being that make us who we are, or about a resurrection from the dead. Once we have laid this groundwork, then I will elaborate on the eternal destiny of every person on earth.

IMMORTAL BEINGS
Many people think we are only physical beings, but that is not true. Man is made up of a trichotomy (three parts): spirit, soul, and body.

1. SPIRIT: Our spirit is the seat of our communion, worship, and communication with God. It is our God-consciousness. It is where the Holy Spirit of God dwells in a born-again Christian and is called *"pneuma."* It is a person's "vertical window" and "the element of faith." I call it our "Headquarters."

2. SOUL: Our soul is our will, intellect, and emotions. It makes up our personality, which is expressed by our words and actions as well as our facial expressions. It is called *psuche*, the immaterial part of man which he has in common with animals. It is our "horizontal window" and is "the element of life." I call it the "Battlefield."

3. BODY: Our body is made up of flesh and bones and is controlled by our five senses: what we see, feel, hear, taste, and touch. It is called *"soma"* and is the element of our physical nature.

The Bible makes this very clear in I Thessalonians 5:23:
*"And the very God of peace sanctify you wholly, and I pray God your whole **spirit**, and **soul** and **body** be preserved blameless unto the coming of our Lord Jesus Christ."* (KJV. Emphasis mine)

We find this truth also in Hebrews 4:12:

*"For the word of God is quick, and powerful, and sharper than any two-edged sword, piercing even to the dividing asunder of **soul** and **spirit**, and of the **joints and marrow** (body), and is a discerner of the thoughts and intents of the heart."* (KJV. Emphasis mine)

A NEW BIRTH
Every person is born in sin; therefore their spirit is dead, separated from God, as it says in Romans 5:12:

"Wherefore, as by one man (Adam) sin entered into the world, and death by sin; and so death passed upon all men, for that all have sinned." (KJV. Emphasis mine.)

This is also expressed by the apostle Paul in Ephesians 2:1:

"And you He made alive, who were dead in trespasses and sins, in which you once walked according to the course of this world, according to the prince of the power of the air (Satan), the spirit who now works in the sons of disobedience, among whom also we all once conducted ourselves in the lusts of our flesh, fulfilling the desires of the flesh and of the mind (soul), and were by nature children of wrath, just as the others." (NKJ)

An unsaved person's spirit is not dead in the sense that it does not function, but is dead to the things of God. It is hostile, insubordinate, rebellious, and controlled by Satan; therefore, it fulfills its lustful desires through the soul (mind) and body, as it says in Galatians 5:19-21:

"Now the works of the flesh are evident, which are: adultery, fornication, uncleanness, lewdness, idolatry, sorcery, hatred, contentions, jealousies, outbursts of wrath, selfish ambitions, dissensions, heresies, envy, murders, drunkenness, revelries, and the like; of which I tell you beforehand, just as I also told you in time past, that those who practice such things will not inherit the kingdom of God" (NKJ)

The apostle Paul is speaking to the Church in the above scriptures, but his words also apply to unbelievers.

The spirit of a person without Christ controls their soul (mind), which in turn controls the body, causing it to perform what the spirit and soul desire. But if a person's spirit is born again (alive and in oneness with God), then the Holy Spirit of God, which dwells in a follower of Jesus Christ, will control the spirit of the person as they submit to Him, which then causes their soul (mind) and body to conform to God's will. The Bible calls this "Walking in the Spirit."

"I say then, Walk in the Spirit, and you shall not fulfill the lust of the flesh. For the flesh lusts against the Spirit, and the Spirit against the flesh; and these are contrary to one another." (Galatians 5:16-17 NKJ)

So, what is the solution for a person whose spirit is dead, separated from God? As there is a natural birth, so is there a spiritual birth when people accept Jesus Christ as Savior and Lord. It is called "being born again." Their spirits become alive in Christ, and the Holy Spirit of God comes to dwell in them, bringing about an *inter-union* and *inter-communion* with God.

The Holy Spirit then begins to direct their lives, teaching them to bring their souls (minds) and bodies into subjection to their spirits so they can live and walk in the ways of God in purity, love, and holy living. This comes by developing a life of prayer, study, and obedience to the principles of God's Word and obedience to Him. The born-again experience is the result of Jesus Christ's shed blood on the cross, His resurrection, and the making of the New Covenant in His blood that we might be saved.

"Knowing that you were not redeemed with corruptible things, like silver or gold, from your aimless conduct received by tradition from your fathers, but with the precious blood of Christ, as of a lamb without blemish and without spot. He indeed was foreordained before the foundation
of the world but was manifest in these last times for you who through Him believe in God, who raised Him from the dead and gave Him glory, so that your faith and hope are in God." (I Peter 1:18-21 NKJ)

The Holy Spirit draws people to Jesus Christ, convicting them of their sin and their need for a Savior. With this conviction, they either accept or reject Jesus Christ, thus determining their future and eternal destiny.

We are immortal creatures who will live forever after death in one of two places—heaven or hell. We get one shot at life on this earth; and who we choose to serve, either Jesus Christ or Satan, will determine where we spend eternity. To be saved, a person must believe in their heart and confess with their mouth that Jesus Christ is their Savior and Lord.

"That if you confess with your mouth the Lord Jesus and believe in your heart that God has raised Him from the dead, you will be saved. For with the heart one believes unto righteousness, and with the mouth confession is made unto salvation. For the Scripture says, "Whoever believes on Him will not be put to shame." For there is no distinction between Jew and Greek, for the same Lord over all is rich to all who call upon Him. For whoever calls on the name of the LORD shall be saved." (Romans 10:9-13 NKJ)

Once a person believes in and confesses Jesus Christ as Savior and Lord, He wipes out their past sins and they become a new person in Him. Regardless of how evil a person has been or what horrible crimes they have committed, when the Holy Spirit brings conviction to their heart, it is God's way of saying, "Come to Me and I will wipe away your past and make you My child." If this is speaking to you as you read this, then it is your time to be born again, to have a new life in Christ Jesus and the promise of an eternal inheritance in His kingdom. This is your moment, your day to change your life, and when the resurrection of the righteous dead happens, you will go to heaven to live forever with God in the most beautiful place ever imagined. It will be a place of total fulfillment, contentment, and peace. There will be much to do, but every activity will be filled with enjoyment as well as God's love and protection.

TWO RESURRECTIONS

When a person dies, the soul and spirit immediately depart from the body and, depending on their relationship with God, will either go to heaven or hell—where evil men and women who denied Jesus Christ as Savior go. The body is buried and returns to dust, but that is not the end of the body. Sometime in the future it will be resurrected and reunited with its soul and spirit in one of two resurrections. First will be the resurrection of the righteous who have gone to Heaven, and will then receive their glorified bodies. Second will be the resurrection of those who have gone to hell to await the final judgment at the end of the Millennium at the Great White Throne when God's books will be opened and each unbeliever judged according to the life they lived while they were on earth: Then they will be cast into the Lake of Fire forever.

Resurrection of the Righteous

The resurrection of the righteous is what is known as the Rapture, or the "catching up" of God's people to Heaven. This will involve two groups. The first group is those who have died before and gone to Heaven. Their dead bodies will be raised and reunited with their souls and spirits, thus becoming glorified saints; then they will be caught up to meet Jesus Christ in the air. The second group will be those who are still alive on earth when the Rapture occurs and will be changed (also glorified) and caught up at the same time. This "catching up" will be made up of all the true saints down through the centuries.

"For this we say to you by the word of the Lord that we who are alive and remain until the coming of the Lord will by no means precede those who are asleep (dead). For the Lord Himself will descend from heaven with a shout, with the voice of an archangel, and with the trumpet of God. And the dead in Christ will rise first. Then we who are alive and remain shall be caught up together with them in the clouds to meet the Lord in the air. And thus we shall always be with

the Lord. Therefore comfort one another with these words." (I Thessalonians 4:15-18 NKJ)

"Behold I shew you a mystery; we shall not all sleep (die), but we shall all be changed, in a moment, in the twinkling of an eye, at the last trump: for the trumpet shall sound, and the dead shall be raised incorruptible, and we shall be changed. For this corruptible must put on incorruption, and this mortal must put on immortality. So when this corruptible shall have put on incorruption, and this mortal shall have put on immortality, then shall be brought to pass the saying that is written, Death is swallowed up in victory. O death, where is thy sting? O grave, where is thy victory? The sting of death is sin; and the strength of sin is the law. But thanks be to God, which giveth us the victory through our Lord Jesus Christ." (I Corinthians 15:51-57 KJV)

The Bible says that followers of Jesus Christ are "strangers and pilgrims" on this earth. It says in First Peter 1:17-19:

"And if ye call on the Father, who without partiality judges according to each ones works, conduct yourselves throughout the time of your sojourning here in fear. Knowing that you were not redeemed with corruptible things, like silver or gold, from you aimless conduct received by tradition from your fathers, but with the precious blood of Christ, as of a lamb without blemish and without spot." (NKJ)

Before Jesus was crucified and resurrected, He made a statement that He would one day return and take His saints to heaven.

"Let not your heart be troubled: you believe in God, believe also in Me. In My Father's house are many mansions; if it were not so, I would have told you. I go to prepare a place for you. And If I go and prepare a place for you, I will come again and receive you to Myself; that where I am, there you may be also." (John 14:1-2 NKJ)

A PREPARED PLACE
The word *"house"* in the previous Scripture is the Greek word *oikia*. It is used to describe the heavenly abode of God and the eternal dwelling place of believers. The word "mansions" is the Greek word *mone* which is related to *monos*, which means *"single, alone." Mone* means "an abode" such as an English manor, a manse, or a mansion. Jesus said there were many mansions in heaven, and there is one prepared for each of those who love and obey Him. The word "place" is the Greek word *topos*, which means "a spot, home, tract." If we interpret this correctly, we can say, *"Jesus has gone to heaven to build, for each of those who love and obey Him, a mansion, just to our liking, in a place called Paradise, on a certain spot, or tract of ground, which He has chosen for us."* How glorious that will be. We will not have to build it; we just move in.

The Raptured saints will go to heaven, move into mansions, and live forever. We will have eternity to explore all of God's heaven and His creation. How will this happen, especially when a person's body is put in the grave and returns to the dust?

One hypothesis is that "every molecule in the human body has a frequency like a serial number. The organisms of the human body possess unique electronic cellular structure. This electronic field is an inherited factor relative to the positive and negative polarity of our ancestors. It has variables relative to the biorhythms (rhythms of periodic cycles of physical and emotional behavior) of our parents so that not only among brothers and sisters does each have his own circuit, but even among identical twins.

In each living cell we all have our own two way transmitter and receiver. There is a second dimension of polarity (electrical) and a third dimension of the biorhythms (electronic). At death, the electrical system goes out first. Then hardware of the physical body decays; but the electronic field of the elements remains in each element. This is how carbon 14 works. C-14 can only work on organic materials; that is why the evolutionists' theory that claims C-14 dating can prove fossils to be millions of years old is a hoax. Fossils are inorganic and C-14 in not applicable to fossils!

Each element of organic decomposition keeps its electronic character. But someone asks, "What if the organic material is cremated?" To do a carbon 14 test, the first thing they do is cremate the organic mass to base carbon. Only then can you get a C-14 readout. The electronic character remains even in the ashes (the blood residue).

When we die the electrical dynamo also dies. However, the electronic numerics of the individual remains in the organic chemistry of that person, even when the body corrupts in the ground and decomposes back to the elements. Those human elements always keep that mysterious electronic numerics in the neutron of the atoms. In Colossians 1:17, speaking of Jesus

Christ, we read, *"He is before all things and by Him all things consist."* (KJV) In the Greek, "All things" is "all neutrons are held together." In Hebrews 1:3, it explains how he holds all the neutrons together. *"Upholding all things by the word of His power."*

We used to think that the atom was the smallest factor in creation, and that the neutron was the core of the atom. Now we know the inside of each neutron is another universe. Hebrews 11:3 says, *"By faith we understand that the worlds were framed by the word of God, so that the things which are seen were not made of things which are visible."* (NKJ)

Since, when we die, our electronic number in our cells remain with our decomposed, decayed, or cremated body, then if the Almighty...who created man from the dust of the earth chooses to *"speak the Word,"* or *"punch in "all systems rise,"* cannot He reconstruct and refurbish His own creation? That is what we call the resurrection."1 We don't know for sure if this is the way God will raise the dead, but it is a possibility.

Resurrection of the ungodly

The resurrection of the saints will take place before Jesus establishes His millennial kingdom on earth, but the resurrection of the ungodly—those who rejected Christ before they died—will take place at the end of Jesus' thousand-year reign on earth.

"But the rest of the dead lived not again until the thousand years were finished...And I saw a great white throne, and him that sat on it, from whose face the earth and the heaven fled away; and there was

found no place for them. And I saw the dead (those who rejected Christ) small and great, stand before God; and the books were opened: and another book was opened which is the book of life: and the dead were judged out of those things which were written in the books, according to their works. And the sea gave up the dead which were in it; and death and hell delivered up the dead which were in them: and they were judged every man according to their works. And death and hell were cast into the lake of fire. This is the second death. And whosoever was not found written in the book of life was cast into the lake of fire." (Revelation 20:5, 11-15 KJV)

At the resurrection of the ungodly, all those who died and went to hell will be brought out to stand before God at the *Great White Throne Judgment* and there be judged according to the life they lived while on earth. Once judged, they will be cast into the Lake of Fire and Brimstone to be tormented day and night forever and ever. Psalm 9:17 says, *"The wicked shall be turned into hell, and all the nations that forget God."*

Hell is a place where there will be no Presence of God, no hope of ever being freed (there will be no bail bond), no joy, laughter, peace, or beauty; no possibility of ever seeing loved ones who have gone to heaven; and, most of all, never being able to experience love again. Those condemned to hell will spend eternity in a state of anguish, being tormented by demons and burning fire, but never burning up. Hell is a place no human being should ever want to go.

There are contemporary true stories of people who have gone to heaven and hell and returned to tell about it. Those who experienced hell made dramatic changes in their lives to avoid going there again. Google "Near Death Experiences" and read people's accounts of both places.

DISCERNING THE LIGHT
There are those who say they have gone to heaven and have even written books about their experiences. But some of their stories do not line up with Scripture. For example, one neurosurgeon claims to have gone to heaven but says that a person does not have to believe any certain way to get there. Then there is the woman, a medical doctor, who has written a book on her experience in heaven; yet in the book she states that she was told that a person does not have to make a decision about whether they want to stay in heaven until after they get there. Both of these accounts violate God's Word. Jesus Christ says of Himself in John 14:6, "*I am the way, the truth, and the life: no man cometh unto the Father, but by me.*" God's Word does not lie, so their experiences must have been counterfeit. But how can a person tell the difference?

How to discern the great light
Dr. Maurice Rawlings wrote a book entitled *Beyond Death's Door.* In it he gives actual accounts of people who have gone to heaven as well as hell and gives some advice on how to discern whether that person has truly seen Jesus Christ and gone to heaven.

1. Satan can disguise himself as an angel of light. (II Corinthians 11:14)
2. Jesus is always identified and will not tell you anything that is contrary to the Bible.
3. The other light is nebulous and does not identify itself.

4. The deceiving light may be forcefully demanding unconditional love for a sinful world.
5. There will be a seeming entrance for all into heaven, regardless of what they believe.
6. There will be no mention of past sins.
7. The light cannot be self-forgiving and just at the same time to those who die, yet have never been saved and forgiven through Jesus Christ and His blood. (I John 5:11-12; Galatians 5:19-21; Revelation 21:7-8.) 2

No one can make you believe in a real heaven and hell, but any thinking person can see that the evidence is overwhelming. If you have any doubts and are searching for truth, then it would be good to do your own research. There is much information, both right and wrong, on the internet regarding people dying and coming back to tell about it. If you will use the seven points above, along with the Bible, you will be able to tell the difference between the true and false accounts.

In our next chapter we will conclude our book with the return of Jesus Christ to earth and the signs that His return is near. If you have not made a decision to follow Jesus Christ, today is the day of salvation, not tomorrow.

Chapter 12
CHRIST'S SOON RETURN

"...Ye men of Galilee, why stand ye gazing up into heaven? This same Jesus, which is taken up from you into heaven, shall so come in like manner as ye have seen him go into heaven." (Acts 1:11 KJV)

SIGNS OF CHRIST'S RETURN

When Jesus Christ came to earth the first time, it was to shed His pure, sinless blood and bring redemption to mankind and all His creation. When He returns the second time, it will be to set up His throne in Jerusalem, Israel—the place of His crucifixion and Resurrection—and take His rightful place as King and Supreme Ruler over the nations of the world. His Coronation in Jerusalem will be greater than any ever experienced on planet earth, as people and leaders of the nations come to celebrate His enthronement and to bow down and worship Him.

The signs of Christ's soon return are evident as prophetic Scriptures continue to be fulfilled at an accelerated rate. Two of these major end-time prophetic events cannot go unnoticed. First is the re-establishment of Israel as a nation after 2,000 years of exile. Second is the soon to be rebuilt Temple on the Temple Mount in Jerusalem. We will examine each of these issues, according to the Word of God and current events, to see how close we really are to Jesus' Second Coming.

THE RESTORATION OF ISRAEL AS A NATION

From the time of the first exile to Babylon to the present time, there has always been a remnant of Jewish people who lived in Israel; but a major event of dramatic proportions took place in 1894 that would forever change their destiny. A Jewish officer in the French army, Captain Alfred Dreyfus, was falsely accused of treason for selling military secrets to Germany. He was convicted without a fair trial and sentenced to life imprisonment on Devil's Island off the coast of South America (In 1898 he was pardoned and in 1906 he was exonerated). At that trial was a man by the name of Theodor Herzl, a newspaper correspondent, who saw the injustice done to his fellow Jew. He then realized that, even though the Jewish people were scattered throughout the world, they were still one people and needed their own homeland.

In 1896 Theodor Herzl published a paper called *The Jewish State* (*Der Judenstaat*) and, in 1897, formed the Zionist Organization, as well as the Jewish Fund and other entities, to collect monies for settling Jewish people in the land of Israel with the dream of having a Jewish State. He also formed the first Zionist Congress and, on August 29, 1897, approximately 200 delegates from 24 countries met in Basel, Switzerland, for the purpose of creating a Jewish State in the land of Israel. Later, Herzl wrote in his diary, "At Basel I founded the Jewish State...Perhaps in five years, and certainly in 50, everyone will know it." His prophecy came true fifty years later, for on November 29, 1947, the United Nations voted in favor of establishing a Jewish State in the land of Israel. There were several events of great importance that led up to the U.N. vote and the reestablishment of the nation of Israel.

The Balfour Declaration

During World War I, Britain was losing to Germany, which had captured the market for the production of acetone, a necessary ingredient for producing arms. It was during this time that a Jewish man by the name of Chaim Weizmann, a chemist and leader of the Zionist movement in Britain, developed a process of synthesizing acetone through fermentation which allowed Britain to produce its own acetone. Acetone is needed to produce cordite, which is a propellant explosive necessary to fire ammunition without generating smoke. It helped Britain win the war and, in doing so, caught the attention of British Prime Minister, David Lloyd George and British Foreign Secretary Lord Arthur James Balfour. They asked Mr. Weizmann what he wanted in return, and he told them he wanted a Jewish homeland for his people in Israel. His request caused the Balfour Declaration to be written by Lord Balfour, stating that they favored a Jewish State in the land of Israel. This was put in a formal letter on November 2, 1917, and sent to Lord Lionel Rothschild, a powerful member of England's Jewish community who carried much weight with the British government.

On July 24, 1922, the Declaration was accepted by the League of Nations but included a mandate that Great Britain have administrative control over the land of Israel. In 1939, Germany started World War II and, due to pressure from the Arab nations, Britain recanted on the Balfour Declaration by issuing the *MacDonald White Paper*, stating that the creation of a Jewish State was no longer their policy or responsibility, therefore they were limiting immigration to Israel. This act fueled the "Holocaust" (a Greek word that means "sacrifice by fire"), which cost the lives of several million European Jews by keeping them from escaping Hitler and Nazi Germany's "Final Solution," whose goal was the total annihilation of the Jewish people. Thank God Hitler did not succeed, although about two-thirds of European Jewry lost their lives. Once again, Satan's plan to eliminate the Jewish bloodline failed.

The end of World War II came in 1945 and, due to the Holocaust, a desire was kindled among many nations to see the Jewish people have their own homeland. As I said earlier, on November 29, 1947, the newly formed United Nations voted to create a "Jewish State." On May 14, 1948, the same day on which the British Mandate ended over the land of Israel, the Jewish people declared themselves a nation again. God's promise to His Chosen People had come to pass after over 2,000 years of exile. Their bloodline and DNA had survived centuries of persecution and enemy plans of annihilation. They were back in the land God had promised them as an everlasting possession (Psalm 105:6-11). The first major sign of Christ's return had taken place.

Middle East Conflict
On May 14, 1948, Israel became a nation again after almost 2,000 years of exile. The same day the first of their wars took place as five Arab nations attacked the newly formed Jewish State with the intention of totally destroying it. They did not succeed.

The second major conflict came nineteen years later on June 5, 1967, with the "Six Day War." It ended six days later, on June 10, and resulted in another Israeli victory and the regaining of the Golan Heights, the West Bank, the Gaza Strip, as well as East Jerusalem, which had been under Jordanian control for nineteen years. Jerusalem was now reunited as the Capital City of Israel.

On Saturday, October 6, 1973, all was quiet in Israel. No transportation services were running, shops were shut down as business as usual came to a halt, and the synagogues were filled with Jewish worshippers. It was Yom Kippur, the biblical "Day of Atonement" and the holiest day in Israel's calendar year. It was a perfect time for an enemy attack.

Unknown to Israel at that time, Egypt and Syria, along with the help of at least ten other Arab countries (through personnel, military equipment, or financial aid) launched an attack on Israel from two fronts: Egypt in the South, from the Sinai Peninsula, and Syria in the North. Their objective was to completely destroy the Jewish nation. The war continued for nineteen days, although Israel was unprepared at the beginning and suffered major losses. Slowly they were able to regroup and, after more than a year of fighting, defeat the Egyptian and Syrian forces. It was a miraculous victory.

The Yom Kippur War was the third major conflict for the Jewish people since they became a nation again.

Spiritual Conflict

From 1967 until today, the Arab nations have been in constant conflict with Israel, consistently trying to destroy her. Many of the world's nations are against her and anti-Semitism is once again on the rise. Why is this? Why, for centuries, have the

Jewish people been the most persecuted on planet earth? To find the answer, we must go back to the Garden of Eden and the bloodline and DNA of Adam and Eve.

After their sin of eating of the Tree of the Knowledge of Good and Evil, God gave Adam and Eve the promise of a future Coming Messiah who would defeat Satan and redeem His creation. Their bloodline and DNA of the godly seed would be passed down to Noah, then to his son Shem, from whose lineage would come Abraham, Isaac, and Jacob and the Jewish people, and would ultimately bring forth the Messiah. It all has to do with the blood covenants God made with them. The persecution of the Jewish people down through the centuries is the result of two things: one, their rejection of God and breaking His covenants; and two, Satan's desire to destroy them. The Jewish people's bloodline and DNA is still of utmost importance because they are the key to the fulfillment of end-time prophecy. Plus, God's plans for them are not yet complete. He ultimately has a glorious future for them.

So the root of the Middle East conflict is spiritual and is being carried out in the physical realm as Satan and his kingdom battle against God and His kingdom. The re-establishment of the nation of Israel and their survival is truly miraculous and a slap in the face of her enemies; but in His Word God said that in the last days, before Jesus Christ returns, He would make them a nation again.

"Who hath heard such a thing? Who hath seen such things? Shall the earth be made to bring forth in one day? Or shall a nation be born at once? For as soon as Zion travailed she brought forth her children.

Shall I bring to the birth, and not cause to bring forth, and shut the womb? saith thy God." (Isaiah 66:8-9 KJV)

Though conflict continues in the Middle East, Israel will survive; for, as I said, there are still prophecies that must be fulfilled.

THE COMING REBUILT TEMPLE

The most important, yet volatile, piece of ground on earth today is the thirty-five acres in Jerusalem, Israel, called The Temple Mount. It is the only place on earth God ever chose to have a building erected for Himself. He gave the plans to King David who, through God's instructions, gave them to his son Solomon so he could build the first Temple. Later, due to Israel's turning from God to worship idols, that Temple was destroyed by the Babylonians in 586 B.C.

The second Temple was built by Zerubbabel, a descendant of King David, when a remnant of Jewish people returned from Babylon in 538 B.C. There was a fourteen-year delay in finishing it, which took from 521 B.C to 516 B.C. In 19 B.C., King Herod the Great, who was an Edomite, restructured, enlarged, and beautified the existing Temple to gain favor with the Jewish people. It was said to be the most beautiful building on earth. It was during its existence that Jesus Christ, at the age of twelve, met with the religious leaders on the Temple Mount and confounded them with His questions and answers. Later, during His ministry, He would teach there. In 70 A.D. the Temple was destroyed by the Romans, and the Jewish people were scattered throughout the world, in what is known today as "The Diaspora."

For almost 2,000 years, Israel has been without a Temple, but when Israel became a nation again in 1948, the desire to rebuild began to grow. In the Six Day War of 1967, Israel regained control of East Jerusalem and the Temple Mount. There was great rejoicing among the Jewish people, as for the first time in eighteen years they were able to access the Temple Mount. The IDF Chief Chaplin Rabbi Shlomo Goren took measurements of its dimensions to determine where to build the Third Temple, but on June 17, 1967, Moshe Dayan, head of the Israeli army, met with the leaders of the Supreme Muslim Council and turned control of the Temple Mount back over to them. Rabbi Goren was furious, but there was nothing he could do about it. God's timing to rebuild was not yet here.

Registering of Levites and Kohanim
In 1978, a worldwide call went out to those with the name of Levi and Cohen to register in Jerusalem in preparation for training of the priesthood and the rebuilding of the Temple. Since then, The Temple Foundation has been raising funds to rebuild. Also, there are at least two yeshivas (training schools for Jewish priesthood) in Jerusalem, Yeshiva Torat Haim and Yeshiva Ateret Kohanim, that are teaching how to conduct Temple services and rituals. Google "The Temple Institute" for more information.

Sanhedrin
On October 13, 2006, the Jewish Sanhedrin was reestablished after over 1900 years. It was the Supreme Religious Court that resided on the Temple Mount in Jerusalem, in the Hall of Hewn Stones, during the Second Temple Period (during Jesus' time). It was called "The Great Sanhedrin," and consisted of 71

members, as does today's Sanhedrin, also called The Great Sanhedrin. Their intention is to rebuild the Temple. Plans have already been drawn up that will be revealed this year, 2013, in Jerusalem by The Temple Institute.

The Priesthood DNA

In 1996, Dr. Karl Skorechi, head of molecular medicine at Technion Institute of Technology in Haifa, Israel (along with colleagues from London, England, and the University of Arizona) conducted a test study to identify the priesthood of the Jewish people. They chose 188 Jewish men from North America, Israel, and England. Dr. Skorechi and his team did not ask the men their surnames but asked if they had been told they were priests. The 68 who claimed priestly descent proved to have a variation of the Y chromosome. Dr. Skorechi says their ancestry dates back to Aaron, the first High Priest who lived 3,000 years ago. This technology was not known until this century. It is amazing that now, after 2,000 years of the Jewish people being scattered throughout the earth they can determine the priesthood for the Temple. Once again, we see the importance of the blood and DNA, passed down from generation to generation through the lineage of Abraham, Isaac, Jacob and the Levitical tribe.

To date, there are about 150 articles prepared for the Temple services, including the golden menorah, cloth for the priestly and High Priest garments, holy anointing oil, holy incense, musical instruments, and the stone altar which is now being built and will be transported to the Temple Mount when it is time.

In Exodus 39:29-30, God commanded that the garments of the High Priest were to be made of fine linen, dyed blue, purple, and scarlet. Also, the cord for the mitre and the tassels on the border of the garments were to be blue. The origin of the method to produce the blue dye was lost when the Muslims invaded Israel in 638 A.D. and forced the Jewish dye industry underground.

Through the investigation of archaeological excavations, the former Chief Rabbi of Israel, Isaac Herzog, found that the dye came from a snail called *Murex Trunculus*. The secret of producing the dye was rediscovered by Otto Elsner of the Shenkar College of Fibers. He found that the hypobranchial gland of the snail, from which the dye was produced, held a clear liquid, which, when exposed to the air, turned purple; but when the shells were crushed to extract the dye and exposed to the sunlight, they turned a brilliant blue.

According the Talmud, the shores of Israel are covered with these snails only once every seventy years. People thought it was an exaggeration, but in late October 1990, it happened. The Ultra Orthodox Jews saw this as a sign of the imminent coming of the Messianic Age, the revival of the priesthood, and the rebuilding of the Temple. They are now using this dye for the first time in 1,300 years for the priestly garments. In Roman times it was valued at $96,000 per ounce, based on today's currency.

Another important dye is the scarlet color which comes from the crimson grub worm (*towla*, in Hebrew), which secretes a crimson fluid that is used as a dye for the High Priest's garments. The story behind this dye is too extensive to put in this chapter, but I would strongly suggest that you Google "crimson grub worm" and go to the site "The Crimson Grub Worm-Insects: Incredible and Inspirational." Read the compelling information there on how this dye is produced.

The only thing remaining for the rebuilding the Temple—other than working out a way to build on the Moslem controlled Temple Mount—is to produce the ashes of the Red Heifer. According to the Orthodox Jewish Rabbis and the biblical text, these ashes are needed to cleanse the Temple Mount (which has been under Gentile control for centuries), as well as cleanse the Jewish people who would come there, due to the fact that they have lived among the Gentile nations and have become defiled. Producing these ashes can be accomplished in two ways. One is if the ashes of the Red Heifer of the Second Temple Period are found. Two is if a Red Heifer is produced that meets all the requirements. Numbers, chapter 19, says the animal has to be without spot (not one hair of another color is allowed) and must never have worn a yoke. Either way, these ashes will be produced soon. Once the ashes are supplied, the rebuilding can begin when the Israeli government gives the go-ahead. At this time they are hindered due to Moslem control of the Temple Mount, the existence of the Dome of the Rock and the El Aksa Mosque, as well as the strong possibility of war breaking out. No one knows how all of this will be resolved, but it will.

The days ahead
Israel becoming a nation again and the soon-to-be-rebuilt Temple are only two of the major last-day prophetic events

spoken of in the Bible. Others are the great increase of evil, the Battle of Gog and Magog, the coming of the Antichrist, and the Battle of Armageddon. Although these are important issues, I will not address them, as my intention for writing this chapter is to give an understanding of the glorious Second Coming of Jesus Christ and the saints' role in returning with Him to earth to rule during the millennium (1,000 year reign).

In chapter eleven, I wrote on the "catching up" (Rapture) of the Church to Heaven. Heaven is a real place of total peace, with no more crying, pain, or death. That will be our eternal home, but that is just the beginning. When Jesus returns to earth at His Second Coming, the saints will come with Him. He will defeat the Antichrist and his armies (see Revelation 17:8-14; 19:11-21; Isaiah 34:1-8; 24:17-23) at the Battle of Armageddon, judge the nations, and establish His kingdom on earth. Not only will we continue to worship and serve Him as our Savior, Lord and King, but the Bible also tells us that we, as His saints, will rule with Him.

"Do ye not know that the saints shall judge the world? and if the world shall be judged by you, are ye unworthy to judge the smallest matters? (I Corinthians 6:2 KJV)

"And he that overcometh, and keepeth my works unto the end, to him will I give power over the nations: And he shall rule them with a rod of iron; as the vessels of a potter shall they be broken to shivers: even as I received of my Father." (Revelation 2:26-27 KJV)

How glorious that will be. Our present time on earth is our training and preparation period for ruling with Him. Our future responsibility and authority depends on how we handle our affairs, our talents, and the material things He gives us here in this life, regardless of how little or how much we have. Some will govern over territories, some ten cities, some five cities, some fewer; however, all of His saints will have their place of rule on earth under Jesus Christ. And do not forget, we will have our glorified bodies and will never die, as will mortals who will be living during the millennium. We will be able to instantly travel from one place to another, even walking through closed doors as Jesus did after His Resurrection.

What about food and recreation? Will we be able to eat, play golf, fish and participate in earthly activities? I do not know about the activities, but we definitely will be eating, just as Jesus did after His resurrection when He sat down to eat with the two men He joined on the road to Emmaus and when He ate breakfast with the disciples on the shore of Galilee. The Bible tells us there will be a "Marriage Supper of the Lamb" when we get to Heaven. What a feast that will be, as saints from every nation on earth gather to celebrate Jesus and their overcoming victory over Satan while on earth.

"Let us be glad and rejoice, and give honour to him: for the marriage of the Lamb is come, and his wife hath made herself ready. And to her was granted that she should be arrayed in fine linen, clean and white: for the fine linen is the righteousness of saints. And he saith unto me, Write, Blessed are they which are called unto the marriage supper of the Lamb. And he saith unto me, These are the true sayings of God." (Revelation 19:7-9 KJV)

Yes, there will be feasting in Heaven, but God will also hold a feast on earth—in Jerusalem, Israel—for all nations during the millennium; and we, as saints, will participate in that, as well.

"And in this mountain shall the LORD of hosts make unto all people a feast of fat things, a feast of wines on the lees, of fat things full of marrow, of wines on the lees well refined." (Isaiah 25:6 KJV)

Words cannot express the joy, peace, love, and eternal bliss that await those who put their trust in Jesus Christ, the Jewish Messiah and Savior of the world. Our time on this earth is like a leaf in the wind compared to eternity. Why not secure your future destiny in heaven now?

Conclusion

At the beginning of this book I stated that I wanted to address several of the most important issues people were seeking answers to, answers of truth and not speculation. Those issues were: Is there a God? Where did evil come from? What mystery does our blood and DNA hold? How could God have a Son without a consort? How could that Son come to earth as a Man? How could His Son, Jesus Christ, be born of a virgin? Why was His DNA so important? Is there proof of His death, burial, and resurrection? How can we be delivered from evil and Satan's kingdom? What are some signs of Christ's soon return to earth? We have addressed each of these accordingly (there is much more that could have been written), with the hope of clearing up misconceptions, both in the secular and religious arenas; yet my ultimate purpose for this book was to touch as many lives as possible, causing them to make an affirmative decision concerning Jesus Christ, thus securing their eternal destiny in Heaven. I believe I have, to the best of my ability and with the help of the precious Holy Spirit, accomplished my goal with valid information regarding each issue. If you are one of those who have been seeking truth and want to change your life, this is your time to make that decision. Below is a prayer you can pray for salvation right now, wherever you are, and be free:

"Dear God, I am a sinner in need of a Savior. I believe, in faith, that Your Son, Jesus Christ, came to earth, lived a perfect life, and gave His pure, sinless blood on the cross for my salvation. I believe that He rose from the dead, ascended to Heaven, and is coming back soon. So I come to you in faith, according to Your Word in Romans 6:23: *"For the wages of sin is death; but the gift of God is eternal life through Jesus Christ our Lord."* And, in Romans 10:9-11: *"That if thou shalt confess with thy mouth the Lord Jesus, and shalt believe in thine heart that God hath raised him from the dead, thou shalt be saved."* Lord, I believe right now. Jesus, I ask you to come into my heart, cleanse me from my sins, and save me. I will serve you the rest of my days on earth."

If you prayed that prayer, let me hear from you. My address is in the back of the book. Also, it is important that you tell others about your decision. If you are a believer in our Lord Jesus Christ, I would love to hear from you, also. May God's richest blessings be yours.

NOTES

CHAPTER 1

1. Josh McDowell, Evidence that demands a verdict (Campus Crusade For Christ, 1972) 24, 25.
2. Ibid., 25.
3. Author unknown.
4. Author unknown.
5. Norman L. Geisler & Frank Turket, I Don't Have Enough Faith To Be An Atheist (Crossway Books, Wheaton, Illinois, 204) 75, 92.
6. Joseph S. Exell, The Biblical Illustrator (Baker Book House, Grand Rapids Michigan) Genesis, Vol. 1, 31.
7. Robin Schumacher, Christian Apologetics & Research Ministry (www.christianeducation.com).
8. Norman L. Geisler & Frank Turket, I Don't Have Enough Faith to Be An Atheist (Crossway Books, Wheaton, Illinois, 204) 172.
9. Ibid., 187.
10. Matthew J. Slick, Christian Apologetics & Research Ministry (Internet, 1995-2012).
11. Higgs Boson, Wikipedia, The Free Encyclopedia (Internet).

CHAPTER 2

1. Henry M. Morris, The Genesis Record (Baker Book House, Grand Rapids, Michigan, 1976) 165, 166.
2. H. Clay Trumbull, The Blood Covenant (Impact Books, Kirkwood, Mo., 1975), 357, 358.

3. Ibid., 358.
4. Ibid., 359.
5. Ibid., 358.

CHAPTER 3

1. E.W. Bullinger, The Witness of the Stars (Kregel Publications, Grand Rapids, Michigan, 1893) 29, 30.
2. Ibid., 31, 32.
3. English Collins Dictionary (Harper Collins Publishers) Internet.
4. www.merriam-webster.com/medical/oxidative520stress.

CHAPTER 4

1. Dr. James Smith, The Promised Messiah (Thomas Nelson Publishers, Nashville, Tn, 1993) 39, 40.
2. O. Palmer Robertson, Christ of The Covenants (Presbyterian & Reform Publishing Co., 1980) 100, 101.
3. Henry M. Morris, The Genesis Record (Baker Book House, Grand Rapids, Michigan,1976) 127.

CHAPTER 5

1. H. Clay Trumbull, The Blood Covenant (Impact Books, Kirkwood, Mo., 1975) Preface V.
2. Ibid., 10, 11.
3. Ibid., 49, 50.
4. Dr. Ed Murphy, The Handbook For Spiritual Warfare (Thomas Nelson Publishers, Nashville, TN, 1992, 1996) 211.

5. H. Clay Trumbull, The Blood Covenant (Impact Books, Kirkwood, MO, 1975) 144, 145.
6. Ravi Zecharias, Ravi Zecharias International Ministries, (Newsletter Update, September 22, 2012).
7. Dr. Ed Murphy, The Handbook For Spiritual Warfare (Thomas Nelson Publishers, Nashville, TN, 1992, 1996) 49.

CHAPTER 6

1. Henry M. Morris, The Genesis Record (Baker Book House, Grand Rapids, Michigan, 1976) 163.
2. Ibid., 174, 175.
3. The Chosen People Magazine (Chosen People Ministries, New York, NY).
4. Josh McDowell, Evidence That Demands a Verdict (Campus Crusade For Christ, 1972) 176, 177.

CHAPTER 7

1. Vines Expository Dictionary (Flemming H. Revell Company, Old Tappan, NJ, 1940) 140.
2. Mark Siljander, Foundations for Discussion on Five Bridges of Unity (email to William Payne "Sonny," August 27, 2003) 3, 4.
3. KJV Study Bible Notes, Zondervan, Grand Rapids, Michigan, 2002) 745.
4. New King James Study Bible Notes (Thomas Nelson Publishers, Nashville, TN, 1997, 2007) 1528.

CHAPTER 8

1. CRUX,Wikipedia, The Free Encyclopedia (Internet).
2. E. W. Bullinger, The Witness of the Stars (Kregel Publications,1893) 48, 49.
3. Ken Ham, Article on Laminin, www.answersingenesis.org.
4. Whirlpool Galaxy, NASA, ESA, www.hubblesite.org/newscenter/archive/releases/2011/031.

CHAPTER 9

1. Josh McDowell, Evidence That Demands a Verdict (Campus Crusade For Christ, 1972) 83.
2. Ibid., 194.
3. Ibid., 194.
4. Ibid., 186.
5. St. Iranaeus, Encyclopedia Britannica web site.
6. Ibid., 205.
7. Ibid. 207.
8. Simon J. Joseph, PhD, Challenging The Disciplinary Divide (Shroud of Turin article, "The Shroud and the Historical Jesus,") Shroud of Turin Website article.
9. Ibid., 6.
10. Leoncio A. Garza-Valdes, The DNA of God (Doubleday, a division of Random House, Inc. New York, NY, 1999) 108-110.

CHAPTER 10

1. Dr. Richard Kent, The Shroud of Turin Prove The Resurrection, (Free Christian Thinking website) 6.

2. Ibid., 7.
3. Ibid., 7.
4. Ibid., 7.
5. Josh McDowell, Evidence That Demands a Verdict (Campus Crusade For Christ, 1972) 198.
6. Ibid., 200.

CHAPTER 11

1. Dr. Reems, The Institute of Judaic Christian Research Newsletter, Vol. 1, November, 1986 (website).
2. Dr. Maurice Rawlings, Beyond Deaths Door (Bantam Books, 1991).

BIBLIOGRAPHY

William L. "Sonny" Payne, Jr., is the Founder and President of New Gate Ministries. He has been in ministry since 1973, having served as a pastor, teacher, and host of a weekly television program. He has ministered in Europe, India and Israel, traveling and teaching God's Word, and has also produced and aired three television specials from Israel. He obtained the first ever television footage of the archaeological excavations at the Temple Mount area in Jerusalem, Israel, dating back to the time of King Solomon.

Sonny has spent over 30 years of in depth study on blood and blood covenanting, and is a learned expositor on Jewish history, the Temple, its sacrifices and the priesthood. His book "Bought With A Price" has been used in schools of ministry, colleges, and churches as an apologetic regarding blood covenanting and the importance of Jesus Christ's blood and resurrection. His desire, and goal, is to see the Jewish people come to know Jesus Christ as their Messiah, and to enlighten the Church on their Jewish heritage.

Sonny and his wife Reva Jo live in Maryville, Tennessee and have two children, a son, Timothy Lee Payne, and daughter, Ami Elizabeth Burr.

Contact information and speaking engagements:

William L. "Sonny" Payne, Jr.

P.O. Box 4764
Maryville, TN 37802

BOOK ORDERS: www.puregoldenterprises.com
Pure Gold Enterprises, P.O. Box 4764, Maryville, TN 37802.

CPSIA information can be obtained at www.ICGtesting.com
Printed in the USA
LVOW101142140513

333630LV00002B/2/P